G
ISLANDS

Travel Guide to an
Enchanting Area

by
Franck Weimert

English translation and adaptation by Dennis Corbyn

TOURBOOKS LONDON

Published by

TOURBOOKS,
Bercourt House,
York Road,
Brentford, Middlesex,
England.

© Tourbooks This edition 1979
ISBN 0-903192-63-2

Original German edition by LN-Verlag, Luebeck
© LN-Verlag 1974

English translation and adaptation by Dennis Corbyn
Series Editor: Yvonne Messenger
Typesetting: Pat Gruenwald

Maps by Dennis Corbyn
Photographs by courtesy of the
National Tourist Organisation of Greece
Cover illustration by Barnaby's Picture Library

Printed in England by
HGA Printing Co. Ltd.,
Brentford, Middlesex.

CONTENTS

3

Spelling of Greek Names

A word of warning is needed about the spelling of Greek place names—a problem which plagues all writers about Greece. When written with English alphabetical symbols, many versions may appear of the same name. For example, Herakleion (in Crete), may also appear as Iraklion, Ieraklion, Heraklion, etc. Furthermore, the Greek form of a well-known place name may be quite different from the English. For example, Athens is Athine on Greek maps, Piraeus is Pireefs, Cephallonia is Kefalinia. To add to the confusion, many well-known places in Greece have acquired a totally different name in English. Corfu Island, for example, is known to Greeks as Kerkira, while Zante is known as Zakinthos and Santorin as Thira.

Insofar as it is possible to keep to rigid rules, the following have been adopted for this book:

Where there is an established English version of a Greek island or town name, this has been used—i.e. Thessalonica has been used rather than Thessaloniki, Cythera rather than Kithira.

Where alternative versions are known, these are given.

Where the Greek town or island name is little known, the version of spelling used is that appearing on maps of Greece, published by the National Tourist Organization of Greece, and obtainable free of charge from their offices.

Changes of name are partly due to the present Greek government's policy of reviving historical names for every-day use. The golden rule is to be prepared for surprises in both spelling and version.

Illustrations Index

Chapter One

ISLAND PATRIOTISM—SOME ARE BORN WITH IT, SOME ACQUIRE IT

It's no exaggeration to say that one fifth of Greece is entirely surrounded by water—for this is exactly the proportion of the land area of Greece that is concentrated in the islands. Put it another way for the northern visitor hungry for sun-soaked beaches: the total length of coastline owned by Greece is about 9,300 miles. And of this 9,300, over 6,800 miles belong to the islands.

In the Aegean Sea area alone there are some 2,000 islands, islets and rocky masses, though it is also true that only about 167 of these are inhabited, or at all habitable. Add to this figure the seven Ionian islands and we get the respectable count of 174 inhabited isles. Yet, surprising though this may seem to those who come from large land areas, every island is a world on its own. To be sure there are similarities, common characteristics, especially among islands from the same group. And it's a weakness of the visitor that he tends to see the unifying factors before he notices the diversity. Yet there's no greater offence you can offer the islander than to compare *his* island

7

with this or that other island. Unless, of course, you first
praise it unreservedly to heaven. . .

Island patriotism is a passion which every Greek Islander
is more or less born with: certainly he imbibes it with
mother's milk. The passion which can befall the northern
visitor is of a different kind: this is *island mania*. This
mania drives him from island to island, until he has assured
himself he knows every one. Starting with the big, tourist-
oriented islands, he progresses to the smaller, quieter ones,
then on to the more remote ones, some twenty hours sail
from Piraeus. Finally, his passion drives him to the tiniest
ones of all, without electric light, without piped water, with
scarcely a human being on them. And only when he knows
them all, will he—like Paris awarding the apple—fix on one
as his favorite. Purged of his island mania, he becomes an
island patriot. And this acquired patriotism often turns
out, in the end, to be even more stubborn than the inborn
kind. . .

Chapter Two

THE IONIAN ISLANDS

The long arm of the Mediterranean which lies between
Italy and the Balkans is known as the Adriatic in the north,
and as the Ionian Sea in the wider part between Greece and
southern Italy. Hugging the Greek coast in this sea are
seven major islands, which have come to be known as the
Ionian Islands, or sometimes, in Greek, *Heptanesa* (seven
isles). Moving from north to south their common names,
in English and Greek, are: Corfu (Kerkira), Paxi (Paxi),
Levkas (Lefkas), Ithaca (Ithaki), Cephallonia (Kefalinia),
Zante (Zakinthos), and finally, Cythera (Kithira)—off the
southern tip of the Greek Peloponnese.

The island group has had a troubled history. After the
fourth Crusade it belonged to the Republic of Venice,
although Levkas fell for a time under Turkish domination. After some further changes of mastery during periods
of the Napoleonic Wars, the islands came under the protection of the British, who established the "United States of
the Ionian Islands". Unlike many of the Greek islands,
the Ionian Islands are all very fertile areas, with lush
vegetation.

9

Corfu—A Fairy-Tale Garden in the Sea

Corfu is the most northerly of the Ionian group, its upper half lying, in fact, off the Albanian, rather than the Greek coast. At its closest point it is only about 1-1/4 miles from the Albanian shore, and for this reason the northern part of Corfu was long a closed military area.

In area about 230 square miles, Corfu has some 100,000 inhabitants. About 30,000 of these live in the capital, which, in Greek, has the same name as the island itself, Kerkira. This name was given to the island as early as 8 B.C. by colonizers from Corinth, but is today used only by the Greeks themselves. The internationally-used name of Corfu is a corruption of the Greek word for a peak— *koryphe*. This relates to the two rocky promontories which are a distinguishing mark of the capital, and formed the basis for a mighty medieval fortress built by the Venetians.

Ships from the powerful Venetian Republic had been accustomed to use Corfu harbors since the start of the 4th Crusade in 1202, and in 1386 the island placed itself under the protection of Venice. Along with the other Ionian Islands, which all gradually accepted the same solution, Corfu remained under this protection till 1797. In this year the islands were taken over by the French, who were eventually replaced by the British. The United States of the Ionian Islands was set up and British influence remained supreme until the mid-19th century. In 1864 the islands became subject to the Greek throne, which had been empty since the abdication of King Otho two years previously. But the King appointed (as George I of the Hellenes), was a British-inspired candidate, and it could not be said that British involvement finally ended till this unfortunate monarch was assassinated in 1913.

Today, there are many ways of reaching Corfu. The quickest way, of course, is by air. New buildings were opened at Kerkira airport in 1973, and traffic is now considerable. Olympic Airways offers a number of flights daily from Athens to the island, and there are also direct connections with London and Brindisi (southern Italy). The airport also has capacity for numerous charter flights.

If you are coming by automobile, the nearest approach from the mainland is via Igoumenitsa. There is a two-hour ferry trip to the island several times a day. A shipping route from Piraeus passes through the impressive Corinth Canal and then proceeds to Corfu via Patras and some stops at other of the Ionian Islands: the voyage may take

up to 12 hours. There is also a shipping line operating from Venice, which makes calls at Corfu—but conditions vary from year to year.

One connection which has been popular for decades is presented by the regular ferry trips from Brindisi to Patras, by way of Corfu. The southern Italian town is pretty easily reached from central Europe by transcontinental motorways (freeways). Also, in summer, it is now served by a number of rail trains with automobile carrying facilities.

The writer can contrast this swift route with his own very first trip to Corfu from a north German center, some twenty years ago. Brindisi then had to be reached by train over an Alpine pass. There followed the long journey down Italy in overcrowded rail cars, and the crossing to Corfu on an ancient Greek steamer in the company of goats, cats and poultry, to say nothing of mountains of passengers' baggage.

Now, scarcely anything remains of those bygone days. In the heart of Corfu town there are still the closely-packed, stately old houses showing an Italian influence, though the pock marks of wartime bombing have now been covered over. Under the arcades of the Spinasa, one of the great public squares of Europe, there are the same old coffee shops, the *kafeníon*; in the big square below the ancient Venetian fortress there are the same old memorials. But the crowd that throngs these places is different. It is a new, exuberant, cosmopolitan crowd, speaking a kind of tormented international English, where previously Greek alone was understood. In fact, Corfu has developed into one of the most popular international holiday centers.

Huge hotel blocks and complexes have arisen around the old town and along the best of the bathing beaches in the vicinity. They seem to strive to offer guests every convenience, without their having to stir an inch from their shelter. But, at the same time, there still remain a few small hotels in the city center to please the individualist with slender means. These establishments let beds, nothing more. Their great advantage, apart from their modest charges, is the fact that they more or less force the guest to come into contact with the locals. He must visit the local shops to find suitable food for breakfast, and is rarely more than a few steps from the Spinasa.

Rarely will you find on any island the same display of luxurious living which is customary evening after evening in Corfu. But, however frequently you may visit one of the luxury hotels, I implore you to take at least one opportunity of slipping away, to spend an evening in the fresh air of the Esplanade, and take a seat in one of the great *tavernas*, under aromatic trees. You will be served by a veritable army of waiters who are not merely diligent, but are genuinely concerned for your well-being.

The best point from which to start a sightseeing tour of Corfu town is the old harbor on the north shore. To the west rise the walls of the New Fortress or Citadel of San Marco, as it is called, built by the Venetians at the end of the 16th century. The great entrance gate is guarded by a fearsome lion of Saint Mark. Close to the wide harbor square, with its taverns, is the Orthodox Cathedral, surrounded by tall houses. Follow Fileninon or Nikoforis-Teodokis Street upwards. You will be astonished by the great numbers of arcades, in which traders display their wares. These arcades serve both to protect from the sun and from the rain—for Corfu has the highest registered rainfall in Greece.

A slender, Roman-style bell-tower will show you the way to the church of Saint Spiridon. This saint was Bishop of Cyprus in the 4th century, and in the 15th century, after the fall of Constantinople, his bones were brought to Corfu. They rest in a golden Renaissance reliquary behind the *iconostasis* in the church (i.e. the icon-hung partition which separates the nave from the altar area), and four times a year are carried in solemn procession through the streets of the capital. This occurs on Palm Sunday, on the night before Easter Sunday, on August 11th, and on the first Saturday in November. (Other celebrated festivals on Corfu are the Good Friday processions, and the Procession of Lights from Mandouki, the north west part of the city of Corfu, on August 14th). Incidentally, the great esteem in which Saint Spiridon is held is shown by the commonness of his name, as demonstrated by the local telephone directory. The first name Spiro also derives from this Saint's name.

From Saint Spiridon's Church it is only a few steps to the Esplanade. In the north west is the imposing arcade erected by the French during their short occupancy, while to the north is the former Royal Palace. This was built in

1862 to house the British Lord High Commissioner, after
the United States of the Ionian Islands had been set up.

To the east, the astonishingly large Esplanade is dominated
by the old fortress, which is now again being put to military
usage. If you have a keen interest in old fortress architecture, you will get permission to look around it with little
difficulty. Some old statues and memorials are reminders
of former British Governors, and of Joannis Kapodistria,
the first Prime Minister of Greece, who hailed from Corfu.

An odd relic of the British occupation is found in the
Cricket Ground off the Esplanade. The British introduced
their national game to the Corfu natives, and a local version
is still played here.

South of the Esplanade and on the right is the Archaeological Museum. Its showpiece is the great Gorgon Pediment
from the Temple of Artemis in the ancient town. Excavated in 1911, this is said to be the remains of the first
carved pictorial scene in the West. In the centre of the
pediment is the giant head of Medusa, flanked on her left
by her son Chrysaor, and on her right by what remains of
the winged horse, Pegasus, her second son. In Greek
legend, the Medusa was one of the three fearful maidens,
known as the Gorgons, whose heads were covered by serpents instead of hair. The look of Medusa was said to be
so horrifying that it turned men instantly to stone.

From the Esplanade a wide avenue leads south along the
coast, then turns right for Kanoni, a beauty spot about
2-1/2 miles distant (buses leave a central point in the
Esplanade for the fortress gate). At the southern end of
the avenue is the town quarter of Anemomilos, with a
number of hotels, and Corfu's favorite beach, Mon Repos.
To the left of the turning for Kanoni is the 12th century
basilica of Aghios Iason and Sosipater. To the right is the
former Royal Summer Palace of Mon Repos, the birthplace
of Britain's Prince Philip, Duke of Edinburgh. It has beautiful grounds, unfortunately *not* open to the public.

It was on this side of the road that the ancient city (known
as Palaeopolis) was located, and it was here that a Corfiote
ploughman first struck the remains of the temple of
Artemis.

A pretty minor road leads to Kanoni, at the tip of the peninsula. Its name (meaning cannon) derives from a former
French battery located here. The view from this high

vantage point is of incredible beauty, and it is justly said
to be one of the finest throughout the world. At the end
of a narrow artificial causeway are the brilliant white
buildings of the Vlachernae convent, and a little farther
on is the tiny islet of Pontikonisi (Mouse Island). According to legend, the islet is the remains of the Phaeacian
ship that finally brought Odysseus home, and was turned
to stone by the angry god Poseidon.

Another excursion can be made from Corfu to the Achilleion. This is a castle-like villa built for the Empress
Elizabeth of Austria in 1891, and passing, after her murder,
into the hands of Kaiser William II of Germany. It now
houses a casino, playing roulette and chemin-de-fer, and
a fine restaurant. The garden, an orgy in green, is well
worth a visit. There is also a room containing mementoes
of the previous imperial owners.

Further south lie a number of large hotels, and the little
resort of Moraitika. Some of the taverns here are to be recommended: in particular, excellent lobster is served at the
right time of year.

Leaving the capital in a westerly direction, you come upon
Glifada, a small resort with a fine beach. To the north west
of Corfu are Kontokali and Gouvia, with their luxurious
hotels and "bungalow hotels". Higher up the rugged west
coast of the island, Paleokastritsa lies in a delightful small
bay embedded in tall surrounding hills. High above the
bay is a 12th century monastery with a fine outlook and a
small museum containing 13th century icons and some
supposed dinosaur bones.

As you leave this monastery you will see one of the many
warning notices erected throughout the islands. This one
simply states: "Aimez les fôrets" (love the woods). It is a
gentle reminder of the appalling destruction that can be
wrought by one carelessly discarded match or cigarette end.
In such an area, a disastrous fire could destroy the work of
decades, of centuries.

The road leading to Sidari, on the north coast of Corfu
island, is generally well made, and, as you finally drive over
the mountain pass leading to the town, you have an enchanting view of little villages nestling in olive woods, a truly
Arcadian prospect. In the villages themselves you will find
tables set out under canopies of vines, and many isolated
corners of unspoiled charm.

Sidari has the same unspoiled air. About 25 miles from
Corfu, it has no sophisticated beach facilities, but a wide,
sandy bay and a number of café-restaurants serving typical Greek food at reasonable prices.

The landscape along this northern coast is impressive. To
the east are the mountains of Albania, to the west, nothing but sea. Continuing in an easterly direction we eventually come to Roda, after a halt in the sleepy village of
Karoussades. The road is poor, but this disadvantage is
greatly outweighed by the continuous magnificent views
of the rich valleys of the island interior—contrasting with
the somewhat bleaker coastline. From Karoussades, a
pretty little wooded road leads to the small beach of
Astrakeris—which is also served by a bus from Corfu
town, during the tourist season. There is a *taverna*
nearby.

But we press on along the road to Roda, pitying anyone
who is forced to drive behind another vehicle on these
mountain-and-valley highways thick with white dust.
Roda is another unspoiled hamlet, with a row of delightful *tavernas* right on the beach itself. On the return
journey you can spare your automobile by driving along
the metalled highway toward Spartylas. This is located
high above the east coast of the island, and affords a
marvellous panoramic view stretching from Corfu town to
the mountain ranges of the Balkans. The road then winds
down to join the route along the east coast. To the north
lies Nissaki, with an excellent beach, and a number of
simple, low-price *tavernas* specializing in fish dishes. Just
north again is Kalami Bay, an untamed camping area with
a shingle beach and the tents scattered in groves of ancient
olive trees. Finally, we should mention Kouloura and
Kassiopi, two further villages up the coast road leading
north. Although, on most maps,'a road is marked connecting up Kassiopi with Roda, the writer was unable to
find this in actuality. Could be, it's still in the planning
stage!

Now, turning to the south to return to Corfu town, we
pass through Ipsos, with its pretty little harbor and rustic
tavernas, then on through Gouvia, showing the remnants
of a Venetian shipyard. On the southern outskirts of
Ipsos a colony of new hotels, bungalow hotels and holiday
homes is springing up.

One treat you must not miss while on Corfu—spend at
least one evening at a local café-bar where *sirtaki* music
and dancing are being presented. Ask the porter of your

hotel which is the current "in" place, and go there (when
the writer last visited Corfu, it was the "Himeromata", to
the west of Mandouki). A fine present to bring back from
your holiday is a set of discs of Greek folk music—you
will both get and give a lot of pleasure with them. Another particular souvenir of Corfu will be a bottle of the
"Corfou" perfume which is distilled here. It is advertised
as "an old gentle Parfume noble sents like the one loved
Corfu-People of the old time. It is superb—Corfu offers it
to remember you. . ."!

Paxi—A Foretaste of the Aegean

If you want an excursion of a completely different kind
while on Corfu, take a trip south to nearby Paxi island:
you enter another world from the lush vegetation of its
northerly neighbor. Paxi, which covers just over 7-3/4
square miles and has about 100 inhabitants, can be reached
by a regular boat service administered by a Corfu travel
office. Sometimes, too, you may have the chance to make
the journey in a *caïque* from Kavos in the south of Corfu.

The only harbor, and the main spot on the island is Gaios,
in the south east. The main spot in Gaios is the harbor
square, and the main characteristics of the island are olive
trees and goats. If you are a guest in a *taverna*, you will
remember it by its excellent goat cheese and the pleasant
flavor of its olive oil—said to be the best in Greece. A clear,
slightly sparkling, non-resinated wine will be served. This
is the product of Antipaxi, a satellite island to the south,
with its west coast lined by vineyards protected by walls.

There is scarcely a better souvenir to bring back from your
holiday than a bottle of Antipaxi wine: the lobsters here are
also excellent, but less convenient to carry!   All-in-all,
Paxi is a spot for anyone who loves small islands and hates
bustle. It has a pleasant little bungalow hotel, directly on
the beach.

Levkas—The 2,600-Year-Old Island

Surprising though it may seem, Levkas is an artificial
island. Until the Corinthians, in 640 B.C., dug a canal
through the muddy isthmus on the east of the "island",
it was joined to the Arcananian mainland. This channel
rapidly silted up and had to be re-excavated—early on,
by the Emperor Augustus and, more recently, at the
beginning of this century.

At its narrowest point, the canal is only a few yards wide, and can be crossed by a street ferry. This is, in fact, the best way of reaching the island, unless you happen to be in your own boat. The writer remembers with mixed feelings his own first attempt to reach Levkas from Ithaca. First, he was obliged to go by *caïque* to the island of Kalamos, to the east of Levkas; the *caïque*-owner was sure he would be able to get a further boat from there. But the wind rose to force 8 to 10: any possibility of continuing to Levkas by boat was ruled out. The next day the *caïque*-owner sailed to the nearby mainland, and the writer accompanied him. There followed an excruciating 30 mile journey, standing in an overcrowded bus, to Vonitsa, then a further journey in an even more overcrowded bus traveling from Vonitsa to the fortress of Santa Maura, which stands directly on the canal separating island from mainland. Here, the writer disembarked, and continued on foot.

But disagreeable though the approach was, I doubt if it was this that gave me an initial impression of Levkas town as a dull place—although the Greek word *lefkas* in fact means "white". But Levkas has suffered greatly as a result of earthquakes in the last few centuries, and this has not helped. This fact, too, probably accounts for the strange way in which some of the small houses have their ground floor continued upwards with a kind of timbering, to form an upper storey entirely of wood.

A new hotel stands before the town—to be recommended as a springboard from which to explore the islands, but not for longer stays. Covering some 116 square miles, Levkas is the fourth largest of the Ionian Islands. It is difficult to see its most attractive aspects without some form of personal transport.

Near the lighthouse on the southern tip of the island is the 236 foot high cliff from which the *katapontismos*, the famed Levkadian Leap, used to take place. This was in early days when a temple of Apollo stood at the spot, and accused persons could prove their innocence if they jumped into the sea—and survived! Priests of Apollo performed the same act as a religious rite, but tied artificial wings to themselves, to help, and were also said to be borne up by flying birds. Another legend claims that frustrated lovers performed the leap, for their own complex reasons, and, in particular that Sappho, the passionate Greek poetess, plunged to her death from this point in an access of despair. The rock is also known as "Lovers' Leap" or "Sappho's Leap".

Following the discovery of some Bronze Age remains at
Nidrion, on the east coast, in 1905, a German archaeologist named Dörpfeld raised the suggestion that Levkas, and
not Ithaca, was the island referred to by Homer in "The
Iliad" as the home of Odysseus. He proposed this in con-
sequence of a passage in the great epic which suggests that
Odysseus's home could be reached over dry land from
Greece, and in spite of the fact that Homer himself refers
to his hero's birthplace as Ithaca. Needless to say, this
theory deeply offended the inhabitants of neighboring
Ithaca itself, but Dörpfeld devoted his whole life to sub-
stantiating it. He died on Levkas in 1940.

In a protected position in the Gulf of Levkas is the small
island of Meganesi: numerous boats from the east coast of
Levkas sail to its main harbor of Vathi, and it has many
quiet bathing beaches. To the north-west, surrounded by
other small islands, is Skorpio. This was the island bought
by the Greek shipping magnate, Aristotle Onassis, in 1962,
and on which, in 1968, he married Jackie Kennedy, the
widow of the American President.

Also to the north west is another private island, Madouri.
It belongs to descendants of the important Greek poet-
statesman Aristotle Valaonitis, who was born in Levkas
and died on Madouri in 1879. As a poet he was much in-
fluenced by Byron, whose name will always be linked with
Greece.

Finally, mention should be made of Vlihon Bay, south of
Nidrion: it is one of the popular holiday haunts of the
island.

Ithaca—Home of Odysseus

The Gulf of Motos, from which a bay leads to Ithaca
port, practically snaps the long, narrow island in half.
In fact, at this point, only a few hundred yards of land
connect the northern and southern parts.

The approach is unforgettable, with sheer walls of rock
on either hand. Then the ship turns south in a right angle
and we enter the Bay of Vathy, leading to the port itself.
This port, the capital of the island, is known equally as
Vathy (meaning "deep"), or Ithaki, after the name of the
island: on Greek maps it generally appears as Ithaki, but
in guidebooks in the English language it is more often
given as Vathy. The name Ithaki comes from a Greek
word signifying "precipitous", and this is as good a

description of the nature of the island as "deep" is of the approach bay.

Some 15 miles long and about 37 miles square, Ithaca has long been generally celebrated as the birthplace of Odysseus, hero of Homer's great epic poem "The Iliad". It has main tained this claim despite some ingenious proposals to the contrary (as mentioned above, under Levkas), and despite the fact that no remains of a Royal Palace of Odysseus have ever been found on the island.

Vathy has some 2,600 inhabitants, and this is about half the population of the island. From here, you can make excursions to every part of Ithaca, and reach numerous good bathing spots. Although Ithaca has not been opened up as a tourist center in the usual sense, it is possible to find good hotel rooms or private accommodation at most times of the year, *except* during the Greek holiday season. At this time—be warned!—you will not find a room for love nor money, unless you have booked in advance. The likelihood, in fact, is that you will find yourself sleeping under the stars—a penalty which, in such a place, has immense compensations. To be candid, there are few sensations more divine than that of waking up under the endless blue sky of Ithaca—where the smallest cloud appears to slink past with a guilty conscience—with the knowledge that yet another day is ready to welcome the island explorer with open arms!

Cephallonia—Sea Mills, Caves and Woods

Since the 15th century there have been some 31 serious earthquakes in the area of the Ionian Islands—a number of them centered on Cephallonia. In the last severe 'quake, in August 1953, 91 per cent of the buildings on the island were destroyed.

Cephallonia (in Greek, Kefalinia), is the largest of the Ionian group and covers about 301 square miles, with a population of around 40,000. Throughout the year, it can be reached by air from Athens, in about an hour, and is visited daily by the ferry from Patras. About once a week there is a call from one of the inter-island steamers connecting with Ithaca, Levkas and Corfu, while smaller ships on the Brindisi-Corfu-Patras-Piraeus route often drop anchor in Sami, the eastern port of the island.

Lying on a long sea inlet on the west of the island is Argostolion, the capital. The city was largely destroyed in the

last earthquake and the modern re-construction has no
very prepossessing appearance. Nevertheless, it has one of
the special tourist hotels of a rather superior class, known
as a *ksenia*, and one or two establishments of categories
C and D. So it can form a good center for exploration of
the island.

Worth seeing in the town itself is the Archaeological Museum, while just outside, on the southern shores of the bay,
are the famed sea-mills—though you may not always find
these in operation. A landmark in the area is Napier's
Lighthouse, taking its name from an English Governor
who was a friend of Lord Byron, at the time of the poet's
sojourn in Cephallonia. Nearby is the outstanding beach
of Platis Ialos, with a good, class A hotel, and the monastery of Aghios Andreas (beautiful frescoes and icons).
Also of interest is the hill village of Metaxata. It was here
that Byron stayed while working on "Don Juan". Close
at hand is the site of the medieval capital of the island,
with the great fortress of Aghios Georgios.

A delightful drive is to take the well-made road leading to
Sami, currently the main port of the island. The road
leads through wooded gorges to the north of the island's
highest peak, Mount Enos (5,250 feet). There is more
accommodation available in Sami, and some good beaches
nearby. It was in this bay that the great naval battles of
Lepanto took place in 1571, when the Turkish fleet was
decisively beaten by the "Holy League" forces commanded
by Don John of Austria.

A great attraction in the neighborhood are a number of
caves with multi-colored stalactites and stalagmites.
Generally, the caves are fitted with electric lighting. When
visiting any, take care not to go without a woollen jacket
or pullover: there is a considerable drop in temperature,
after the warm sun outside. A particular natural wonder
is the Lake of Melissani, a deep cave with a lake and an
opening to the sky, which produces rainbow reflections
when the sun is at its height.

If you take the road north from Sami, you will pass
through Aghia Efimia, a popular yachting harbor, on the
way to Assos, on the north-west coast. Here there are some
fine houses, dating back to a fortress built here by the
Venetians in 1595. On the northern tip of Cephallonia is
a picturesque little village called Fiskardon. It has earned
a place in history as the burial place of Robert Guiscard,
a Norman prince who conquered the island in 1085.

Across the bay from Argostolion lies Lixourion, and to the
north of the town, the remains of Palli. This was the original ancient settlement in the area, and gives its name to the
whole of this appendix-like north-western peninsula. Other
ancient remains (names given in brackets), will be found
near Argostolion (Krane), Sami (Same), and south-east of
Mount Enos (Pronnoi). The island's patron saint is Gerasi-
mos. A few miles east of Mazarakata, there is a monastic
foundation in his name. On August 16th and October 20th
each year this is the scene of heavily-attended pilgrimages.

A final word on Argostolion. In the museum we have mentioned you will find archaeological remains from throughout the islands, and especially items of jewellery, tools and
vases taken from graves dating from the Mycenaean civilization of 1600-1100 B.C. On a technical note, it appears
that one reason the nearby sea-mills currently find operation less easy is that the whole surface of Cephallonia was
lifted by some eighteen inches during the 1953 earthquake,
so that the same volume of water no longer enters to turn
the mills.

Zante (Zakinthos)—The Flower of the Levant

"Flower of the Levant" was the title given this particularly
beautiful island by the Venetians, during their period of
sway over the Ionian group. Zante, more often found in
English texts, is the Italian name.

Some 25 miles long by 12-1/2 wide, the island covers
an area of 154 square miles. Known for its gentle climate
and fertility, it produces wine, vegetables, grain and superb
olives: it is the equal of the better-known Corfu in scenic
beauty.

There are many ways of getting to Zante. The quickest, of
course, is by air—there are year-round flights from Athens
by Olympic Airways (thrice weekly). By sea, there is a
ferry from Kilini on the mainland several times a day, the
trip lasting about 1-1/4 hours. Kilini can be reached by bus
or train from Athens—a somewhat time-consuming business.
The ferry docks in the harbor of the capital, Zakinthos,
overlooked by a hill on which once stood the island's Acropolis, now only the remains of a Venetian fort.

About a quarter of Zante's population of 40,000 live in the
capital: it also has most of the island's hotel accommodation. Before the disastrous earthquake of 1953, Zakinthos

was considered an architectural jewel. But though the loss of so many fine buildings is sad, the modern town offers many attractions. First and foremost, perhaps, the Museum, which houses a rich collection of paintings, icons and iconostases rescued from the disaster.

As far as art treasures are concerned, Zante profited surprisingly from Turkish marauding in the sixth century. After the Turks had conquered Crete in the latter half of the century, many skilled Greek painters flocked to Zante. It was not merely a matter of protecting their faith, but their livelihood. They feared the Turkish hatred of any kind of imagery would force them to paint nothing but decorative friezes, and fled to a kindlier cultural climate. So Zakinthos developed into an art center, much encouraged by its contact with Venice and the broad European tradition of the day.

Pre-earthquake Zante had some 60 churches: almost all were destroyed. Among the survivors, partly restored, partly freshly built, are Phaneromeni and Kiria ton Angelou from the 17th century, and the church of Saint Dionysius, patron saint of the island. The saint's feast is celebrated on August 24th and December 17th each year, with fireworks and elaborate ceremonies.

Worth looking at in the capital are the memorials to two Greek poets, Dionysos Salomas and Andreas Kalvos, who were of great significance in the development of Greek literature. Salomas, born on Zante in 1798, was highly educated, but chose to write hymns and epic poems in Popular Greek, rather than the High Greek of which we will speak later (see chapter in **The Greek Language: A Little Help**). In this respect, he broke emphatically with tradition. Kalvos, born on Zante in 1792, wrote odes in a somewhat antiquated style. Both poets are highly regarded by the modern Greek.

Some pleasant excursions can be made from Zakinthos. The best beaches are Tsilni (2 miles); Alike (3 miles to the north-west); Laganas (6 miles to the south-west); Argassion (3-3/4 miles); Porto Roma (7-1/2 miles to the south-east). Sights to see are the monastery of Paneia Skopiotissa on the 1,300 feet high Mount Skopos, giving a fine view of the island; the Blue Grotto of Zakinthos, with magical light reflections; the village of Kerion, on the south-east spur of Zante, with its pitch sources, used in caulking fishing boats.

If you're staying longer in Zante, try the hotels in Argassion and Laganas: there is also a small, class D hotel in Alike. All these have one advantage in common—proximity to the beach.

Zante's festivals are known throughout Greece, and you will have difficulty in getting unbooked accommodation at the Orthodox Easter or on either of the feasts of Saint Dionysius.

Cythera—Bridge Between East and West

This 107 square mile island forms a sort of bridge between the Ionian Sea to the west and the Aegean to the east—yet it is counted as one of the Ionian group.

Before the cutting of the Corinth canal, Cythera was of great importance to mercantile shipping. The earliest settlers here were the Phoenicians, who set up extensive purple dye works on the island, thanks to the presence of the purple snail in the area. Among the ancient Greeks, the tradition held that Aphrodite, goddess of love and beauty, rose from the sea in the neighborhood of Cythera.

By way of Kastri, on the Bay of Avlemonas, you can take a road inland which leads to the site of the ancient island acropolis—the hilltop fort-cum-shrine which formed the center of primitive Greek communities. Cythera's Acropolis consisted of two shrines, each on a hill; a little lower was the shrine of the goddess Aphrodite. The drive from the capital is particularly scenically beautiful.

Cythera is not an island for everybody, and it doesn't attract much tourist trade. First and foremost, it is difficult of access: shipping connections from Piraeus are irregular, and can last up to twelve hours. There are better ferry connections from Neapolis and Githion on the mainland—but both these towns are themselves difficult to reach by public transport (the easiest way is from the town of Sparti).

The simplest approach to Cythera during the summer months is by air. The little 18-seater aircraft which flies here regularly from Athens is almost always fully booked. The main harbors for the island are Aghia Pelagia in the north-east, and Kapsalion, close to the capital, Kithira, in the south of the island. Smaller type hotels and/or private accommodation may be found in these places.

The capital's museum holds remains from a Minoan settlement here in the second century B.C. They were found in recent years on the site of the ancient capital, above Avlemonas Bay. There are sandy beaches along the shores of Kapsalion Bay, and especially of Avlemonas Bay. But, for the most part, the island's coasts are fairly precipitous, making it a popular venue for underwater fishermen.

Chapter Three

ISLANDS OF THE ARGOLIC AND SARONIC GULFS

Thanks to a good overall transport network, the islands lying in the Saronic and Argolic Gulfs, to the south-west of Athens, have become favorite excursion spots for Athenians. But they are also suitable for full-scale holidays, and some of them, in fact, have become fashionable resorts.

Salamis—The Island Suburb of Athens

Lying in the north-east corner of the Saronic Gulf, the proximity of this 37 square mile island to Athens makes it almost a suburb of the Greek capital. It is easily reached by ferry from Perama, a few miles north-west of Piraeus. The ferry port is also easily reached by bus and street-car connections.

Early in its history (6th century B.C.) Salamis was the object of a dispute between Athens and the nearby town of Megara: both cities wanted the island for strategic reasons. The dispute was finally settled by the celebrated

Athenian legislator, Solon, and it passed into the hands of
Athens, so assuring the safety of their port, Piraeus. But
the island is chiefly memorable in history as the site of the
decisive battle between the Greek and Persian fleets in
480 B.C. The Persians, under Xerxes, attacked with over
1,000 ships, the Greeks having only some 400 to oppose
them. But the Greeks lured their enemy into shallow and
tricky waters off the coast of Salamis, where only they
knew the tides and channels. The defeat of the Persian
fleet was shattering, and decisive for the history of the
western world.

Today, there are some good hotels on the island, especially
in Selinia and Eantion. Over half the island's population
of 20,000 live in the capital, Salamis. It is a good starting
point for a visit to the monastery of Vaneromeri, about 4
miles to the west, where you will find some beautiful
frescoes dating from 1725. Close to the monastery there
are some good camping spots, as elsewhere along the coast.

Aegina—With the Lowest Rainfall in Greece

Aegina (Egina on Greek maps), stands bang in the center
of the Saronic Gulf. It is quickly reached from Athens by
steamer or, in the summer months, by the Hydrofoil
Express. This easy access has caused Aegina to become
a favorite holiday spot for Athenians—either for a flying
weekend visit, or for longer periods.

The island is well equipped to cope with its visitors, having
a plethora of hotels, from luxury class to the least expen-
sive. The two most frequented spots are the capital,
Egina, and the little east coast holiday resort of Aghia
Marina. The latter is easily reached by bus from the capital, and has excellent beaches. Perdika, on the south
coast, also has good bus connections with Egina, and has
some enchanting little bays within walking distance.

Aegina is certainly outstanding for its sea-bathing facilities,
but this should not blind us to the momentous past of
the island. Its central position in a wide gulf ensured that
its was the subject of early occupation. In fact, the first
settlements here were as early as 3,000-4,000 B.C. By
1,000 B.C., the little island had already become a commercial republic, so important and so advanced that in
650 B.C. it minted its own coins—the first European state
to do so. In the Persian-Greek wars it first sided with
Persia, but at the battle of Salamis supported Athens.
Nevertheless, Athens was nervous of the potential menace

of the island, and in 430 B.C. conquered it, and ordered
the people to destroy their fortifications.

Many years of insignificance followed for the island.
From 1540 to 1821 it was under Turkish domination.
During Greece's struggle for independence in the last
century, the island was, for a time, the home of the Greek
government, under its Prime Minister Kapodistrias. Later,
the seat of government was shifted to Athens. A memorial
to this troubled period is Kanaris's house, to the north-
west of the outer harbor jetty: Kanaris was a hero of the
Wars of Liberation. From this point, too, in calm weather,
you can see the remains of the ancient harbor wall under
the surface of the sea.

Worth visiting in Egina is the Museum, close to the cathedral: it contains some fragments of the ancient temple of
Aegina and some fine ancient ceramics. On the road to the
famed Temple of Aphaia you will find, to the left of the
road, the remains of Palaeochora, which was the medieval
capital of the island. All the houses have been demolished,
their stones serving as building blocks for fresh homes
nearer the sea. Only the churches, more than twenty of
them, mostly from the 13th and 14th century, remain, as
a reminder of what the town once was.

The Temple of Aphaia, above Aghia Marina, is one of the
most famous of Greek antiquities. It was built in honor of
the goddesses Athene and Aphaia, at the time of Aegina's
commercial splendor. Of the 32 columns which originally
composed the Cella, or Great Hall of the temple, in which
the huge effigy of the god or goddess was placed, only 25
remain, together with parts of the cross-beams and 7 of the
10 pillars which formerly divided the·Cella into three naves.
The reconstructed sculptures in the pediment show battle
scenes from mythology, the original stonework having been
removed to various museums.

The highest peak of the island, Profitis Elias (also called
Oros), is about 1,740 feet high, and can best be ascended
from the village of Marathon. This village is easily reached
by bus from the capital (about 3-3/4 miles). It will take
you 2-3 hours and a good deal of perseverance to reach the
top, where there is an ancient Temple of Zeus. But the
splendid view, to the mainland of Attica on the one hand,
and the Peloponnese on the other, is worth the effort.

Poros—Poseidon's Isle

The name Poros denotes "passage-way" and there could
be no better description of the narrow straits which divide
this little island from the mainland: they are only some
270 yards wide. The opposing mainland town is Galatas.

Poros covers about 9 square miles and has some 5,000
inhabitants—most of these living in the capital, also called
Poros. It is directly opposite Galatas, at the narrowest
part of the straits. Like Aegina, the island has excellent
connections with Athens, ships calling several times daily,
with the Hydrofoil Express service in summer.

On the east coast, Poros has a naval college and a harbor
for larger ships. There are creeks suitable for bathing to
the north, and some ideal sandy beaches on the western
coast—the latter being well protected from summer storms.

The island is noted for its pine and lemon groves, and
many business men from Athens and central Europe have
built holiday homes here. But there is also a series of good
hotels, for which advance booking is absolutely essential in
the summer months.

From the capital, a rewarding excursion can be made by
way of the monastery of Zoudochou Pigi (containing remarkable iconostases and icons of Mary) to the ruins of
the Temple of Poseidon, dating from the 11th century B.C.
According to tradition, it was here that the great Greek
orator, Demosthenes, took his life in 332 B.C., to avoid
capture by troops of the Macedonian King Antipatros. Unfortunately, little remains of the temple, which was a significant gathering spot before the rise in importance of
Aegina Island.

Poros is an ideal base for trips to the mainland. In particular, an interesting excursion can be made to Damalas, a
small village not far from Galatas, and close to the site of
the ancient colony of Troezen. According to legend,
Troezen was the birthplace of Theseus, Prince of Attica,
who conquered the Minotaur and abducted the Princess
Ariadne from Crete to Naxos. In 1823, the third Greek
National Assembly had its seat in Damalas, and it was during
this term that Kapodistrias was elected Prime Minister.

Hydra—A Breath of Italy

At least one Greek historian has said that credit for the liberation of Greece from Turkish oppression was due in large measure to the fleet of ships supplied by Hydra (known as Idra in Greek and Ydra in some English texts). And one look at the fine old houses formerly occupied by the island's sea captains will certainly convince a visitor that these men were counted of more than ordinary importance.

Hydra achieved no special significance either in ancient times or the Middle Ages. Its place in history begins with a legend dating from the 17th century. It is said that, about the middle of this century, when the Turks were again plundering the Greek coasts, two of Hydra's eminent citizens begged the marauders at least to spare the monastery of Pangia and its icons of Mary. The Turkish reply was to arrest the pleaders and deport them to slave labor in a shipyard in Crete (then under the Turks' control). But the two citizens eventually returned to their homeland and set about teaching the islanders all they had learned about the construction of seagoing vessels. It is said the islanders' first efforts were pretty crude, but at length Hydra became not only a Greek shipbuilding center, but also a focal point for trade. Albanian immigrants brought new blood to the island, and helped in "running" the British blockade during the Napoleonic Wars.

So the 19th century began on a wave of prosperity for this barren and virtually tree-less little island. Legend even has it that the Hydrians used gold pieces as ballast in their ships! At any rate, when open revolt against Turkish dominion broke out in 1821, Hydra was able to put a force of some 150 converted merchantmen into the struggle, to accompany ships from Psara, Chios and Spetsaï.

Today, the names of the old sea-captains who headed the struggle are immortalized as the names of countless streets and boats—Miaoulis, Tombazis, Psamados, Kountouriotis—you will see them frequently. Likewise many of the mansions of the old *kapetanaioi* are still occupied by their descendants; some can be looked over. A branch of the Academy of Fine Arts is housed in the former residence of Admiral Tombazis.

The capital is characterized by narrow alleys and flights of steps. After its heyday in the 19th century, the town fell into decay, until it was revivified by the tourist trade. It is now a favorite center for globetrotters and, especially, artists. Much about the town reminds one of Italy,

especially southern Italy or even Capri. The harbor is a
real jewel, with a little anchorage in the west, and farther
west still a good bathing beach.

Many travel writers recommend climbing the 1,600 feet
high Mount Idra, just behind the town. You get a magnificent view, as far as Sifnos and Serifos of the Cyclades
group of islands.

Spetsaï—And a Breath of Luxury

Spetsaï (Spetse in Greek) is one of those privileged islands
which can be reached by airplane as well as ship. By sea,
it can be reached from Piraeus, though with time-consuming
stops at Aegina, Poros and Hydra: in the peak season, much
faster by motor boat. By air, the island is a short hop from
Porto Cheli (in Greek: Porto Heli) on the mainland.

In antiquity, Spetsaï was known as Pitioussa (island of
pines). But despite its favorable position, it achieved no
special significance. It first appears in history after the 4th
Crusade, when Catalans, Genoese and Venetians all strug-
gled for its possession. Like Hydra, it profited from
Albanian immigration, and became the port for a large
merchant fleet. Many early 19th century captains' houses
testify to this period of prosperity, when some 15,000
people lived on the island.

Spetsaï, too, made a significant contribution to the wars
of liberation from the Turks, sending a fleet of some 100
ships to join battle. In the September of every year since
1822 the despatch of these vessels is ceremoniously remembered in an "Armada Memorial" service in the church
erected to celebrate the victory.

After the administrative centre of United Greece shifted
from Nauplia (Greek: Nafplion) to Athens, and Siros Island
and Piraeus became important trade and shipping points,
Spetsaï began to decline. Much of the population left
for Athens or emigrated to the United States. It is only
since the turn of the century that the fortunes of the
island have again risen. Spetsaï developed into an exclusive holiday resort for rich Athenians, and, after World
War I, into an international resort. Major tourist facilities
have been built in Spetse, the capital, which is now well
established in the modern holiday trade. Nevertheless, in
the ubiquitous fragile-looking horse cabs which largely
dominate the city traffic, it retains some of the charm of
its more recent past.

Spetsaï is too far from Athens to be satisfactory as a day's excursion—a fact that has actually helped the island to stand on its own feet. Among food delicacies it offers are fish dishes *à la Spetsiosa* and pheasants from the neighboring Spetsopoula Island. As far as bathing facilities are concerned, Spetsaï has numerous delightful spots—and these are often quite deserted outside the peak season.

Chapter Four

EUBOEA AND THE NORTHERN SPORADES

Known to modern Greeks as Evia, Euboea Island has become a favorite holiday haunt of the Athenian—partly because of its extensiveness and beauty, partly because of its proximity and easy access. But it is also steadily acquiring an international acclaim as well.

Better known internationally are the northern Sporades to the east of Euboea—namely Alonnisos (caution! also sometimes known as Iliodromia in English texts), Skiathos and Skopelos. The best-known and most-frequented of these is Skiathos: the other two still have something of a reputation for being isolated.

Euboea—The Only-Just-an-Island Island

The second largest of the Greek Islands (the first is Crete), Euboea is, in fact, only just an island. The Atalanti Channel, which separates it from the mainland of Boeotia and Attica is so narrow, at one point, that it is spanned by a short bridge! Nevertheless it is, geographically, an island and covers some 1,380 square miles, with a population of over

160,000. It is about 90 miles in length, varying in width
between 4 and 30 miles. The island is also sometimes
known as Egripos, or as Negropont, and it figured impor-
tantly in ancient Greek history, especially during the periods
of Graeco-Persian wars. It became subject to Athens in
446 B.C., then in 338 A.D. was conquered by Macedonia.
It then fell successively under Roman, Venetian (Middle
Ages) and Turkish rule. Finally, in 1832, it was reincor-
porated in a United Greece.

The proximity of Euboea to the mainland guarantees easy
travel access. Apart from the bridge crossing at Chalkis
(Halkis), the capital, there are ferry crossings from mainland Arkitsa to Loutra Edipsou (every 2 hours); from
mainland Skala Oropou to Eretria (hourly); and from
mainland Rafina to N. Stira, Marmarion or Karistos
(current frequency of ferries not known—but not so
frequent as the others). There is also a direct rail connection from Athens to a mainland station immediately
opposite Chalkis.

The shortest of these ferry links from the mainland is that
landing at Eretria. Once the great rival of Chalkis, this is
today a peaceful bathing resort, with a fine beach and
hotels. Of interest in the neighborhood are the little
museum and the remains of the ancient theater. This
latter will be of particular interest to the playgoer, for it
is only here that a direct connection is preserved between
the stage area and the orchestra area. With the help of
simple apparatus, this enabled a character (often a god or
goddess) in the drama to appear quite suddenly on the
stage—leading to the expression still used in drama writing,
deus ex machina.

Moving south from here along the good coast road, we
pass a number of beach-side hotels, and reach Amarinthos,
then, eventually, at the easternmost end of the island,
Karistos. Unless it is unavoidable, this long drive should
not be made when tired or when the sun is at its peak, for
magnificent though the constantly-changing views are,
the relentless succession of bend after bend demands the
greatest concentration on the part of the driver. Nevertheless, the beauty of the scenery and the character of Karistos
will make the effort seem worthwhile. For Karistos is a
peaceful little town, so far undiscovered by the foreign
tourist, where Greeks on holiday take their ease in rustic
guest-houses or under the awnings of sleepy waterfront
tavernas.

The return journey will have to be made over the same route, with a diversion at Lepoura to visit Kimi on the northern coast. First and foremost, this 25-mile drive is one of the most beautiful on the island, and, secondly, this little town clinging to the hillside is well worth seeing. It stands near the site of the ancient settlement of Kyme, which fathered the Greek settlement of Cumae near Naples in Italy. There are buses from Chalkis and even from Athens to the harbor of Paralia Kimis, just south of the town, a real beauty spot. Unfortunately, it has no sandy beach. The only tourist class hotel is the Aktaion, a few yards left of the entry of the road into the harbor area.

Loutra Edipsou, the ferry terminus at the north-western end of the island, is Euboea's best-loved health resort. Even in Roman times, its waters were celebrated for their healing effect in cases of rheumatism, arthritis and gallstones. It is really the tourist center of Euboea, with a wide choice of hotels of all categories. By road, it is about 60 miles from Chalkis. The first half of this drive is scenically magnificent. You pass through beautiful deciduous forests and deep gorges of reddish rock like Alpine passes. Somewhat after Prokopion the road crosses a wide plain area, with ancient trees and a winding stream. On summer weekends you will see entire families from Athens picnicking here— a picture of bucolic peace.

A left turn off this road at Strofilia will take you quickly (in about 12 miles) to the little coast resort of Limni. This is a favorite spot on a steep part of the coast, but with good bathing beaches and some pleasant *tavernas*. At any time other than the hottest part of the summer it is an excellent center from which to organize rambles or walking tours.

It should, in fact, be said here that Euboea is walking country *par excellence*, especially in the northern part. But one aspect which must not be overlooked is that one must not expect to find here the sort of organized, marked routes you might meet in some National Park or Nature Reserve. Nor will you find available the sort of large scale map which will enable you to pinpoint your position at any time by studying the features. If you go for a walk of any length, select some outstanding feature or landmark—a group of trees, perhaps, or the summit of a hill or mountain—which will enable you to orient yourself and find the way back when the time comes!

Almost finally, I must recommend one excursion which is child's play as far as orientation is concerned—and that is, a climb to the 5,700 feet summit of Dirfi, the island's

highest mountain. Start out from Chalkis, following the
north-east road for about 4 miles to Artaki. Here, fork
right, and pass through the villages of Pissonas, Katheni
and Steni (about 20 miles). From here on, it's all on foot.
East of the last village, a continuously winding path leads
up through woods to a *col* between the summit and the
neighboring peak of Xerovani. The main path now goes on
up for about another half mile in continuous serpentine
bends, reaches the tree-line—the highest point at which
trees grow—and then, shortly afterwards, the ridge leading
to the summit. The view from the top is breathtaking. The
whole of Euboea lies at your feet, and beyond that, the
wide Aegean, with its multitude of islands.

Last of all, a word to bathing fans. If sea-bathing is your
passion, don't miss a visit to Gialtra Bay, west of Loutra
Edipsou at the north-west tip of the island. There is a fine
area of sandy beach here, with some thermal springs.

Crossing to the Northern Sporades

Paralia Kimis, the port of Kimi on the east coast of Euboea,
is a kind of focal point for shipping services connecting the
northern Sporades with each other, and with the mainland
port of Volos (north-west of northern Euboea). The
easterly island of Skiros is also touched by a line travelling
from Piraeus to Thessalonica, while the westerly island,
Skiathos, is on a line traveling between Thessalonica and
Volos.

If you are traveling from Athens, your journey will have
plenty of variety! Leaving the Greek capital by automobile or bus, take the freeway to the port of Skala Oropou
(already mentioned): this is a drive of some 37 miles. From
this port there is an hourly ferry to Eretria on Euboea.
After disembarking, travel east to Lepoura (25 miles), then
branch north for Kimi. From here, a fascinating, twisting
road takes you down to the port of Paralia Kimis.

Skiros—Achilles's Isle

If you ever studied Homer, you may remember how the
island of Skiros appears in the story of Achilles. Thetis, the
mother of Achilles, hearing how the oracle had prophesied
her son would die, if he went to fight at Troy, put him in
women's clothes and hid him in the court of Queen Deida-
meia of Skiros. By means of a ruse, Odysseus detected the
young man, and he went to Troy to become a national hero
and die there.

Skiros (sometimes spelt Skyros), is the largest of the northern Sporades: it covers some 80 square miles and has 3,000
inhabitants. The number and quality of its sandy beaches
is a byword. The capital, on the east flank of the isle, is
also called Skiros—as so often in the Greek Islands. But in
this area, the locals have a common name for all capitals,
calling each one the *chora* of the island. In Skiros, it lies
at the foot of a steep, mountainous hump, where the Dukes
of Naxos formerly built their forts. From this point there
is a magnificent view over the capital, and you will see how
most houses have their roofs covered with thick layers of
sand, as a protection against the fierce sun.

A saunter through the steps and alley-ways of the town
will show you how the island has achieved a relative prosperity. Not being blessed with over-fertile land, the locals
have relied on handicrafts for their livelihood. Their
elaborately carved "Skiros furniture" is known throughout Greece, likewise the china-ware, plates and curious
jugs which are made here.

In the south-west of the island is Krebuki Bay. Here, in
an olive grove, are the remains of the English poet, Rupert
Brooke, who died on the island in 1915, at the age of 28.
His best known work was a sonnet beginning:

> "If I should die, think only this of me:
>   That there's some corner of a foreign field
>   That is for ever England. . . . "

An idealized nude statue of the poet, in bronze, stands in
the capital.

As will be mentioned under **Nude Bathing** in the **INFOR-
MATION A-Z** section, the idea of nudity is still somewhat
repugnant to the modern Orthodox Greek. But if your
penchant is in that direction, Skiros has many miles of
coastline so isolated that none will care whether you enter
the water clothed or unclothed.

Alonnisos—The Green Island

This island covers about 23 square miles and has some
1,000 inhabitants. The travel agents praised it so unceas-
ingly as "secluded" and "unspoiled by the tourist trade"
that now, of course, it is just the opposite: it is as thronged
as any other island—by tourists in search of seclusion! Ad-
mittedly, however, those who come to Alonnisos are not

so much the Jet-Set, as discerning visitors who know just what this island has to offer.

The same-name capital of Alonnisos stands on a 660 feet eminence close to the south-western tip of the island. It is the highest point there is, and affords a splendid view. Most accommodation available is in the harbor-town of Pattitiri, but there are also some good, native hotels in Votsi and Steni Valla. The island is little blessed with roads or mechanical transport, and the best beaches are reached by boat from Pattitiri. From here, too, you can reach the neighboring islet of Perestiri, on which only a handful of people live.

Skopelos—And the Jewel of the Aegean

This little island covers less than 40 square miles and has only about 5,000 inhabitants. Nevertheless, although no remains are now visible, there is evidence that there were settlements here in Neolithic times, and, later, a Minoan colony.

About 3,000 of the population live in the capital, Skopelos, on the north coast. Looking at the little town, with its multi-storeyed houses clinging to the side of a hill, with its medieval citadel, one can well understand why it has been named "the jewel of the Aegean". The second largest town, with about 1,500 inhabitants, is Glossa, in the south-west, with its nearby harbor, Skala Glossas (also known as Platanas).

Either from this latter harbor, or from the capital, it is possible to reach many delightful bathing coves. There is private accommodation available throughout the island, although the hotels are concentrated in the capital.

One advantage which Skopelos shares with Alonnisos and Skiathos is that—in contrast to the Cyclades and most Aegean islands—it is relatively thickly wooded. This means, of course, there are great opportunities for pleasant hikes and rambles.

Skiathos—The Island of Beautiful Beaches

Don't be taken in by the above title. It's quite true that this island has the finest beaches, and what is more—

relative to the length of coastline—the most of them. But the fact is that all these beaches have been well and truly "discovered" by the tourist, and—like the tables in the restaurants, the rooms in the hotels and guest-houses, the seats in the aircraft—they are constantly beset by visitors.

Half an hour by air from Athens, Skiathos is the last island in the chain of the northern Sporades, and only some three miles from the mainland. It can also be reached by ship from Thessalonica, Volos or Paralia Kimis on Euboea. The first thing that strikes you when you enter the harbor is how different the houses here are from the cubic houses on the Cyclades Islands. Here, they are taller, and are uniformly fitted with red roofing tiles. The harbor is split into two basins by the little rocky islet of Bourtzi. The larger, East Basin, is for vessels from the main shipping lines; the picturesque West Basin shelters *caïques*, fishing boats and yachts.

The town of Skiathos, with a population of 3,000, is the only unified community on the island. It was founded after 1825, in the spot previously occupied by the ancient harbor town—which had remained for centuries uninhabited. In the troubled Middle Ages, the people of Skiathos had withdrawn to the mountain town of Kastro, on the northeast point of the island. Today, Kastro molders entirely deserted, atop its 160 feet high crag. Its ruins make a good goal for an outing—it can be reached by boat, or after a 3-hour long footslog across the island. Skiathos is, by and large, a green island, covering just over 20 square miles, and is ideal for walks and rambles. The writer met a number of English people who had settled on Skiathos and knew every nook and cranny, including the numerous monasteries which are becoming more and more deserted, due to lack of postulants.

The beaches of Skiathos are celebrated, and none more so than that of Koukounaries Bay, about 7 miles south-west of the town: many claim it is the finest beach of the Aegean. It can be reached either by boat or bus from Skiathos town. A few hundred yards behind the bay there is a lagoon: along its northern shore the road runs on to a further beach on the western side of the island. Here, it is often calm, when the water in Koukounaries Bay is quite rough. To the north-east of here lies Mandraki Bay, also connected to Skiathos town by bus, or reachable on foot. It is particularly suited to diving, and enchants visitors with its white sand dunes—an unusual sight in the Aegean.

There are also good beaches along the Kalamaki Peninsula,
especially Tzaneria Bay, Argyrolimnos and Kulios.

If you intend to stay any length of time on Skiathos, the
best plan is to start by making a complete tour of the island
by boat. This will give you the chance to spot the beaches
most likely to offer what you want. There are also excellent
beaches on the neighboring islets of Arkos and Tsougrias.

Finally, a word about one of the best-known sons of
Skiathos Island. The poet Alexander Papadiamantis,
known as "the saint of Greek Literature" was born here
in 1851. Don't miss a visit to the house in which he
once lived: it is only a few steps from the harbor. The
house lies in the midst of the charming tangle of narrow
streets which constitute Skiathos town. You will find
some pretty *tavernas* and garden-restaurants, as well as
good quality—if not exactly cheap—handicraft and antique
shops.

The writer's happiest memories are of the harbor cafés,
especially east of Bourtzi. It is delightful to sit at one
of these early in the morning, shaded from the sun by
the wide awning, and be served with breakfast, with the
cubes of butter swimming in little pots of honey, in the
true Skiathos style.

Chapter Five

THE NORTHERN AEGEAN ISLANDS

Three islands comprise this small group in the north of the
Aegean Sea, just before the Dardanelles: the wooded isles
of Thasos (in Greek: Thassos) and Samothrace (in Greek:
Samothraki), and the fertile central island of Limnos, which
has its own airfield. Thasos and Samothrace are best reached
from the mainland of Thrace. The islands lying farther east
in this area belong to Turkey.

Thasos: A Green Wonderland of the North

Kavala, on the mainland, is the best point from which to
reach this green island where sea, sky, rock, mountain and
glen seem to blend in one of the most entrancing of Greek
landscapes. There is an airport at Kavala, to which there are
regular flights by Olympic Airways, while from the port
there is a regular steamer service to Thasos. If you arrive at
Kavala by automobile, you will do best to travel on a few
more miles to Keramoti, and take the car ferry from there.

Thasos, covering about 150 square miles, and with a population of 16,000, is the most northerly of the Greek Islands. Its proverbial fertility, mild climate and excellent harbor have all contributed to giving it a special place since ancient times.

Politically, Thasos belongs to Greek Macedonia, and is administered from Kavala. The outstanding qualities of the island plus its proximity, make it a favorite resort for the people of Thessalonica. With ideal sandy beaches it combines a wide range of hotels rated from good to very good. Its highest peak, Mount Ipsarion (4,000 feet), can be climbed in only four hours from the town of Thassos, on the northern coastline of the almost circular island.

Thassos, the capital, also known as Limenas, has a population of 1,900. It stands at a point where there has been a settlement since ancient times, and to which colonizers from the island of Paros (in the Cyclades Group) once came. Like Paros, Thasos was once celebrated for its marble—in fact its 2-mile long, partially-preserved town wall, dating from 400-500 B.C., is built from marble: some relief work is cut into the gateways, which served as little shrines. To the north there is a Temple to Dionysus, beside the path to the shrine of Poseidon; to the east, the shrine of "the foreign gods". South of this last shrine is the ancient theater, while a path leads up to the former Acropolis, with the remains of a Temple to Athene and a medieval citadel. Without fail, visit the small museum: it has some remarkable exhibits, including statues and a strange sphinx.

A ring road circling the island is approaching completion at the time of writing. Worth looking at is the town of Limenaria in the south-west of the island, with some 2,000 inhabitants, and the former loading point for the zinc and copper ores found on Thasos. Inland from here is the picturesque township of Theologos, where some 2,000 people live.

From this point a minor road leads to Potamia, set among orchards near the east coast. In this village a custom prevails which will be found in other communities of the island—namely, that a special type of cake is baked in honor of any person who has recently died. If you are offered such, have no scruples about accepting it.

Near to this village is its harbor, Skala Potamias, with fine sandy beaches nearby, sometimes with dunes backed by luxuriant olive groves. About 1-3/4 miles to the north is another beach to be recommended, in Kemenarias Bay.

The ring road continues through the pretty little village of Panagia to the bathing resort of Makriammos, just 1-1/4 miles south-east of the capital.

Samothrace—And the Secret of the Ruins

The distance (some 230 sea miles) from Piraeus makes Samothrace one of the most remote of all the Greek Islands. It first became part of Greece in 1912, together with Imbros, to the south-east—though this latter island later reverted to Turkey, to whom it still belongs.

The long haul from Piraeus takes some 20 hours—and, as you can well imagine, it is not generally the most up-to-date and comfortable ships which are deployed on such a little-used line. There are also occasional ship connections from Thessalonica or Kavala, also about once a week from the southerly neighbor, Lemnos. From the port of Alexandroupolis, on the north Greek mainland, there is a boat service at least three times a week, while Alexandroupolis itself may be reached by bus from Thessalonica, or by air from Athens. You land on Samothrace at Kamariotissa harbor—in itself no small ordeal in rough weather.

Once you have landed, you find yourself on an island that is unique in almost every way. The mighty, 5,500 feet high mountain which dominates Samothrace seems to rise directly out of the sea. This is Mount Fengári, the highest peak in the Thracian area, apart from Mount Athos. According to Homer, it was from this height that the god Poseidon chose to watch the Trojan War. It was Homer, too, incidentally, who first called the island Samo-Thrace (meaning Thracian Samos), to distinguish it from the larger island of Samos to the south.

Today, some 4,000 people live on the 70 square miles of the island. Of this number, about 1,500 inhabit the capital, Samothraki, which lies 3 miles inland from Kamariotissa. If you are staying in Samothrace during the summer months, when the peak of Fengari is free from snow, you should not miss the opportunity of attempting to climb it. At the same time, experienced climbers warn the writer, this should not be undertaken without proper equipment and the services of a guide. If you are determined to try it, your best plan will be to ask in the capital if any local person would be willing to accompany you. The magnificent view from the top is said to be ample reward for the labors of the climb.

But it's equal
without ar
densel
the r
a

y possible to see the beauties of this island
ything like such strenuous efforts. There are
wooded areas to the east and in the north. Also in
orth is Therma, a tiny little place of pilgrimage, where
ery popular Festival of Mary is held on August 9th
each year: as the name suggests, there are also curative
springs here. Experienced travelers have also told me there
are first-class beaches on the western and south-western
coasts of Samothrace.

But the island's main claim to fame lies in the archaeological finds which have been made. The area of the excavations is about 3-3/4 miles from Kamariotissa. It was
close to here that the celebrated "Winged Victory", now
in the Louvre, Paris, was found in 1863. Since that time,
French, Austrian, and latterly, American archaeologists
have continued to dig. Many interesting objects have
been brought to light, though not all have been entirely
explicable. Much evidence indicates that Samothrace was
colonized from the island of Lesbos—but also that the
original language here was Thracian and not Greek. This
fact accounts for much of the mystery surrounding inves-
tigation of the Temple of Samothrace. One thing, at least,
is clear—that this "Sanctuary of the Great Gods" was
counted of the greatest importance in antiquity. The
city established by the colonists from Lesbos remained
until the days when Christianity became the Roman State
religion. It was replaced by a village, which lasted till the
15th century. Now, only a mole remains to mark the largely
silted up old harbor. There is a small hostelry here, if you
wish to remain any length of time (reserve in advance).

Worth seeing in the vicinity are the ruins of the ancient
city walls: they give some idea of the importance the place
once had. At the same time, however, it must be empha-
sized that the main significance of Samothrace was in the
religious rather than the political field. The cult of which
the island was a center is linked with the *Cabiri*, a set of
mystic divinities, possibly of Phoenician origin, who were
extensively worshipped in the ancient world as fertility
gods and were represented by phallic symbolism. These
gods were also invoked against shipwreck—appropriate
enough at this point in the Aegean, where the currents of
the Dardanelles make themselves felt.

The anchorage is dominated by two Genoese castles. The
museum is located on one of the fortified hills, from which
a road leads inland. The main excavations are found on a
rise on the left hand side of the water course. The most
important is the *Anaktoron*, a huge reception hall. On the

north side a raised part was divided off, with two giant statues of the gods (*Anakes*). Only the initiates (*mystes*) of the cult had access to this area. Built onto the south-east is a small chamber, a sort of sacristy, in which sacred inscriptions were kept. Close by is the *Arsinoeion*, built by Queen Arsinoë II of Egypt after her marriage to King Lysimachus of Thrace. With a diameter of some 66 feet, it is one of the largest (formerly) roofed rotunda ever found from this period.

If you now go a little farther in a southerly direction, you will reach the *propylon* (entrance hall) of a *temenos* (sacred precinct). Formerly, a frieze of dancing girls ran around the room at eye level: this is now partly on view in the museum. Joined to the *temenos* are the remains of a further shrine, the so-called *hieron*, dating from the 4th century B.C.: it has much of the appearance of a Christian chapel.

Limnos—Vulcan's Isle

Whatever way you reach Limnos, by sea or by air, its effect is overpowering. Aircraft land in the south-east of the island; ships anchor in Mirina Bay, off the west coast, and passengers are taken ashore in small boats.

The island, also Limnos in Greek, sometimes Lemnos in English texts, covers about 175 square miles, with a 1,400 feet peak, Skopia, in the north-west. It has been known for its fertility since ancient times, when it was considered the granary of the Aegean. In recent years, grain production has been largely ousted by cotton growing as an industry, as a particularly high quality cotton thrives in the area. Like most of the islands, Limnos is also proud of its honey—but the Limnosians are prouder than most, for legend has it that theirs was the only kind allowed to be set before the gods of Olympus.

Limnos has its individual enthusiasts—I met visitors who regularly come here year after year—but it has not become a major tourist attraction in the modern sense. But this doesn't mean you won't find comfortable accommodation. On the contrary, a luxury bungalow hotel was built here a few years ago, on the beach to the north of the capital, while there are numerous hotels in categories C and D in the capital itself, and in Moudros. There is also plenty of private accommodation, and, recently, some holiday homes—which can be rented—have been erected.

The capital is Mirina, by the west coast anchorage mentioned. But locals have their own name for the town—Kastro. It is dominated by a medieval fort, from which there are some fine views. After the conquest of Constantinople in 1204, Limnos first belonged to a Venetian family, and then to the Republic itself. Later, the island was re-conquered by the Byzantines and given in fiefdom to the Genoese branch of the Gateluzzi family. In the 15th century the Turks occupied the whole island and it did not become part of Greece till 1912.

A good area of the island for sandy beaches is the southwest: they can be reached from Mirina on foot. There are also good beaches south of Moudros, though these are not to be recommended for small children, owing to the frequent roughness of the water. There is a regular bus service from the capital to Kontias, another good beach area.

Those interested in archaeology and pre-history will find much to fascinate them on Limnos, including the exhibits in the museum in the north of the capital. To visit the archaeological sites thoroughly, however, you must either have a great deal of time to spare, or your own transport. There is an automobile hire firm in the main street of Mirina—but, in the peak season, you will need to advise your requirements well in advance!

In the east of the island, reached by way of Livadori, Rossopouli and Kaminia (at this point, make enquiries about the sparse rocky path), are the remains of a prehistoric Aegean settlement, the town of Poliochni. Here, over an area measuring some 100 by 200 yards, Italian archaeologists dug up the foundations of a town which had existed between 1,700 and 3,000 B.C. A writing tablet, now in the museum, shows a language akin to ancient Etruscan. Likewise a ceramic found at Hephaista, the next archaeological site, shows a close connection with the Etruscans.

The Hephaista site is not easy to find. It stands on a silted-up arm of an inland bay off the Bay of Pournia in the north-east of the island. It is best reached from the village of Megas Alexandros, being about 3 miles south-west of the village over field paths. The town that stood at the spot first appeared around 8 B.C. and was destroyed by the Turks in 1395. No major excavations have so far been carried out here. On the western side of Pournia Bay a fortified watch tower was built on the ruins of an ancient, abandoned town. Today, a Chapel of Mary stands on the spot (there is a fresh water point down some 50 steps below the chapel).

A final spot of archaeological interest is the Kabir Temple at Kloi, on the eastern side of the inland bay. It was found by diggers early in the '60s, and comprises traces of a shrine believed to belong to a pre-Greek mystery cult. As at the Poliochni excavations, a custodian is on duty all day here, and will (almost) break his neck in an effort to impart the secrets of the remains to the rare visitor.

But we have still not mentioned the most famous legend of all connected with Limnos, and which gives it its second name of "Vulcan's Isle". It was held, in Greek mythology, that Hephaestus, (better known in English as Vulcan), a son of Zeus and Hera, was twice flung down from Heaven by one or other of his angry parents. On the second occasion he landed on Limnos, not surprisingly breaking both his legs in the fall, which had lasted an entire day. Thereafter, Limnos was regarded as a special favorite of this god, who was venerated as the deity of fire, and also of smiths, metal-workers and artificers. A more rational explanation of this legend is that Limnos was earlier than most parts of Greece in the practice of metalworking.

Another legend concerns the "Limnian Misdeeds". After Vulcan had made Limnos his favorite spot on earth, he married Aphrodite. She, however, proved faithless, and the good women of Limnos, indignant at the cuckolding of their protector, refused to render the goddess her due worship. Enraged, Aphrodite smote the Limnian women with a combination of under-arm odor and bad breath—so bad, in fact, that their husbands would not come near them, but sought solace among the women of Thrace. Now it was the turn of the Limnian women to be furious, and they assaulted and massacred the entire adult male population. Things might indeed have been bad for the future of Limnos. But just then, as fate would have it, who should happen by but Jason and his sturdy Argonauts, in the course of a long and woman-less voyage. Sailors being sailors everywhere, they fell to with a will, cheerfully ignoring both B.O. and bad breath, and after a short stay had left enough children behind to ensure the future of Limnos for many generations. Or so the legend goes. . . .

Chapter Six

THE EASTERN AEGEAN ISLANDS

Owing to their proximity and also their geological kinship
to the central mainland of Asia Minor, these islands in the
eastern part of the Aegean Sea are sometimes called the
Asia Minor Islands. By contrast with the Cyclades Group,
they are very fertile in parts, and also are generally more
wooded. Their development as tourist centers is still in its
infancy—but Chios, Lesbos and Samos, at least, have regular air connections with Athens.

Lesbos—Where Sappho Sang

The best way to get to know the reality of life on the
Greek Islands is, of course, through conversation with the
inhabitants. This is not easy. It means either the traveler
must know Greek well, or have the good fortune to meet
an islander with a good knowledge of his own language.
But if you *are* able to converse with the natives, you may
be sure of pleasant surprises. Above all, you will meet that
overwhelming island patriotism, which makes the islander
stop at nothing in unfolding to you all the mysteries he

knows of his own island—for this is his world, or at very
least, the center of his world. The writer had this pleasant
experience on Lesbos, where the son of his hotelier spared
no pains to show him all that was worth seeing on this
lovely and ancient island.

Lesbos (Greek: Lesvos) was for many years known universally as Mytilene (Greek: Mitilini), and this is the
name you will find in airport directions and air timetables. But the Greek government is now making efforts
to restore the ancient names, and you will find Lesvos on
Greek National Tourist Organization maps, and in official
literature.

Lesbos is the third largest of the Greek Islands—after Crete
and Euboea—with a total area around 630 square miles.
Lying in the jaws of a large bay off the western mainland
of Turkey, Lesbos was Turkish from 1462 till 1913. One
can, in fact, still sense a breath of the Orient, as one arrives
in the capital of Mitilini, lying on a picturesque gulf in the
south-east of the island. With a population of 26,000,
the city has harbor facilities for large ships, combined with
good accommodation facilities, a bathing beach, and
another good beach at nearby Kratigos, to the south.

The island itself has a total population of some 118,000,
making it one of the most densely peopled areas of Greece.
It offers some entrancing landscapes. Although I toured
the entire island, covering every grade of road in a hired
automobile, I would add that this is not essential. If the
reader will concentrate on the excursion goals I outline in
the following paragraphs, he will find that most can be
reached over good roads starting from Mitilini.

The first goal to mention is Mithimna (also called Mólivos)
on a northern tip of Lesbos, reached via the coast road
from the capital. Your first halt could be at Thermi
(official name: Loutropolis Thermis), a resort with a good
number of hotels. Close by is an excavation site with the
remains of a prehistoric settlement.

Continuing up the coast road for some 20 miles, you come
to the Bay of Aghios Stephanos, where there is a magnificent beach with a *taverna*. The journey continues through
endless olive groves—the olives of Lesbos have been famous
since antiquity. Lesbos is also know for its excellent
wheat, grown in the southern part of the island.

For my own part, I took the worse road from here on,
leading round the north flank of the island. But I would

recommend anyone who wishes to spare his automobile to bear left at Kapi, and return to the coast road at Petra. The remarkable thing about this little village is the small church perched atop a rock rising from the midst of the houses.

From Petra it is about another 4 miles to our goal, Mithimna (population 2,000). Although it is dangerous to indulge in superlatives when talking about the Greek Islands, I have no hesitation in naming this as one of the most delightful townships in the Aegean. There is a good beach, and at the end of the motor road, a picturesque fishing harbor. Above it, the little town seems to grow from the very rock of the sheltering hill, topped by a powerful fort.

There is an attractive walk up the hill from the beach level. By way of some wide steps you reach the narrow "high street", where there are a few *tavernas* and some coffee and souvenir shops. A little higher, you get an unencumbered view of the gloomy walls of the castle. A few more narrow alleys and steps, past some sparse-looking gardens, and you reach the old castle entrance, with a crumbling wooden door still creaking on its hinges. After the color of life below, it seems almost as if you are stepping into some grim film of the past, with a stern reality of harsh, uncompromising battles. At this point the Turkish enemy was only some 6 miles away across the straits. And it was to check them that the Gateluzzi family from Genoa built this fort—eventually in vain, for the Turks took it in 1462.

Another good trip from Mitilini is to take the main road which goes straight across the island to Sigrion on the west coast, a journey of some 60 miles. In the first half of this trip you will get a good idea of the fertility of the island, and will also see the two long inlets of Kolpos Gheras (8-3/4 miles long by 3 miles wide) and Kolpos Kallonis (13 miles long by 5-1/2 miles wide). Also on this route is the great Roman aqueduct at Lampumili, and the salt flats of Kaloni, to the right of the road.

By way of Vantoussa, you come to Antissa, built close to the site of one of the ancient cities of Lesbos. From here on, you enter a bizarre mountain world, with volcanic rock heaped up like the waves of a frozen sea. In the later part of the day this produces light effects of a strange charm. The road now winds down to the Bay of Sigrion, with its pretty beach and inviting *tavernas*. A small hotel is open here during the summer months.

If you now continue south-east to Eressos, you will pass
a sight unique in Europe, a row of petrified tree trunks
some 700,000 years old. They are trees which have been
covered with volcanic ash during an eruption and have
then become petrified as a result of various chemical
changes. As the surrounding volcanic layers wore away
over the course of centuries, the old tree shapes emerged,
some of them as much as twenty feet high. During the
time of the writer's visit, the Sigrion-Eressos road was
only partly open: if this should still be the case, when
you visit the island, go at least as far as Tsichlion Gorge,
to see this remarkable phenomenon.

But, on your return journey to Mitilini, make a detour,
if necessary, to see Eressos, if only to visit its fine beach
at Skala Eressos. On the site of the present community
once stood the ancient town of Lesbos, in which Sappho,
the world's first and perhaps greatest poetess lived.
Roundabout 600 B.C. Sappho was conducting a pre-
marriage school for rich and high-born young ladies—a
sort of exclusive finishing school in which pupil-teacher
relations evidently went beyond the bounds of pure edu-
cation. At any rate, Sappho's poems described female-
female love in such passionate terms that the term lesbian
has been applied to it ever since. In one of the greatest
literary tragedies of all time, Sappho's poems were burned
by the ecclesiastical authorities in 1073, but sufficient
fragments remain to establish their high quality.

Another trip to recommend from Mitilini is a visit to the
village of Agiassos, about 20 miles to the west. It is a large
village (4,000 inhabitants) and lies on the northern side of
the island peak of Mount Olympus, which can be climbed
from this point. The village is also known for its potteries
and spinning work. In the 19th century main church of the
village is a wonder-working Icon of Mary, to which thousands of pilgrims stream from all over Greece, on August
15th each year, the Feast of the Assumption of Mary.

Chios—Island Pride and Island Sorrow

Chios is the home of most of the leading Greek ship-owners,
all rich men, and Greece holds a foremost place among the
sea-faring nations of the world. Therefore, as the geome-
trician would say, Chios must be a rich island.

You can sense this in the course of that Greek institution
known as the *volta*, the evening stroll. You get the

unmistakable feeling of the pride of these people in their riches, their presence, their reputation.

Nevertheless, the writer's first encounter with this sense of reputation was far from pleasant. I had come from Turkey with nothing but a load of goodwill, plus the usual documents, proofs of inoculation, etc. But it seems these documents and jabs were still not good enough for this "proud island", and I was not allowed to land. However, after much discussion, I was allowed to visit an island doctor who— after keeping me waiting some two hours or more—eventually let me go, *without* the required jab, but at least *with* the all-important rubber stamp.

Still, there are always compensations, and this unfavorable start led to my making the acquaintance of one of the best hotels in the Aegean, which—contrary to usual practice— I both name and warmly recommend. This is the Chandris Hotel, on the south-east side of the harbor basin of Chios, the capital. Though officially ranked as category B, I've no hesitation whatever in describing it as the most comfortable and best managed hotel I have met in the Aegean. As my subsequent stay there proved, the quality of both food and service could hardly be excelled. It was only some time later that I realized that Chandris is the name of an important ship-owner, who is now diversifying in the hotel range.

As mentioned, this hotel constitutes the south-east corner of the harbor; to the north is the *kastro*, a large Genoese building of interest. A mile or two to the north is the outer suburb of Vrondados, its "villa splendor" now somewhat outmoded, but nevertheless with a fine beach. To the south of this colony there is the Stone of Homer, a chunk of rock which reputedly marks the birthplace of the poet—who, indeed, very likely came from Chios, though not necessarily from this spot. Kardamila, near the north coast of the island, is said to have the strongest claim to be his actual birthplace.

On one occasion, Homer refers to this island as "the rocky realm", and that seems particularly applicable to the northern, and especially the north-eastern part of the island. Nevertheless, when approaching the wild and inaccessible slopes which constitute the area, it is surprising to see the lushness of the vegetation, especially at the lower levels. Ascent of the 4,250 feet high Mount Profitis Elias gives magnificent views, but will take some four hours. The ascent can be made from either Spartunta on the west coast, or from Vitian on the north coast. But what *must* be recommended is that you procure as detailed a map of the area as possible—or even a local guide. Furthermore, when on the way, neglect no opportunity to check up with local people that you are on the right track. I well remember once asking an old man the way in a small mountain village of Chios. Eventually, the entire population turned out to give me advice, and at least four different routes were recommended. At the time it seemed almost a grand opera performance, but on reflection I realized it simply showed how intensely people here feel about everyday occurrences.

About 5-1/2 miles west of the capital is a sight which should have a high place in a list of "musts". This is the monastery of Nea Moni, which can be reached in a good two hours on foot, or by bus from Chios town to Karie, followed by two miles on foot or by taxi. Nea Moni—the name means "new monastery"—is, despite manifold destruction in the course of its eventful history, a fine example of Byzantine architecture. It owes its existence to a prophecy. When Constantine Monomachos, a Byzantine general and pretender to the throne, was in exile on Lesbos, three monks from Chios prophesied the overthrow of the then ruler of Byzantium. Later, Monomachos became Emperor (1042) and, in gratitude, founded the monastery at this spot, where there had been a wonder-working Icon of Mary. The monastery became very powerful, governing two-thirds of the island—and though it has suffered much from earthquake damage, still contains Christian mosaics of international repute. Those preserved show sixteen scenes from the life of Christ, as well as representations of Saint Anne, and of the Virgin Mary, and other saintly figures. Date of foundation of Nea Moni was probably the middle of the 11th century. At the height of its power, the monastery sheltered some 800 monks, now it is kept in order by only a few nuns. They will show you the old refectory, and also the cistern and charnel house, in which lie the skeletons of several thousand Christian believers who were victims of a Turkish massacre here in 1823. After the appalling carnage of that year, only some 6,000 remained of the former 100,000 inhabitants of the island.

There are some similar bone-yards to be seen in other parts of the island, as, for example, in the monastery of Aghios Minas to the south of the capital.

For centuries the prosperity of Chios was founded on the cultivation, sale and export of gum mastic. This substance, obtained from the resin of a wild shrub (*Pistacia Lentiscus*), was highly prized by the courtesans of antiquity, as well as by Turkish harem ladies, as a kind of chewing gum. It improved the smell of the breath and was also said to have aphrodisiac qualities. If you wish to test this, you can still buy portions wrapped in cellophane on Chios today.

Another way mastic is taken is as a spoonful of sticky fluid in a glass of water. The mastic is sucked from the spoon and the whole washed down with water, to remove the clinging taste. This offering is known as a "submarine" (*ypovrichion*). But perhaps the favorite way for foreigners to absorb mastic is in spirit form, as the drink *mastika*, a mild-tasting but potent liquor.

The mastic-producing districts are mainly in the south of the island, and the villages of Pirgion, Olympi and Mesta are celebrated in this respect: all can be reached by bus from Chios, leaving from Platia Vunakis, close to the quayside.

The best-known of these villages is Pirgion, mainly because of the delightful ornamentation of the houses by the *sgraffito* technique of scratching through a surface to reveal a colored ground. When visiting the town, don't miss a visit to the town citadel to the left of the main square, and the 12th century Byzantine Church of Aghii Apostoli, hidden behind the houses. About 5 miles to the south-east are some excavations of a pre-historic settlement, dating from neolithic times. This is at Emporion, on an east coast bay.

Samos—A Glint of Paradise

Ships from Piraeus make two landings on Samos—first at Karlovassion to the north-west, then 12 miles east, at the capital town of Samos. The ancient capital lay close to the present-day fishing village of Pythagorion, on the south-east coast, and less than a mile from the Turkish mainland.

Whether you arrive by ship or plane, the first impression of Samos is the same—of a huge mountain chain stretching clean across the island in an east-west direction. This chain is dominated in the west by the peak of Mount Cerceteus (Greek: Kerkris), rising to 4,670 feet and in the east by Mount Ampelus (Greek: Ampelos), of some 3,800 feet. The name *ampelos* means vineyard. About ten per cent of the island is used for viniculture—producing the well-known sweet and light Samos wine.

The island has been occupied since about 3,000 B.C., but according to legend, was overrun by Greek nomads from

Cephallonia around 1,000 B.C. Among famous historical
figures from the island was the tyrant Polycrates (5th century B.C.), who formed the subject of a famous ballad by
Schiller, "The Ring of Polycrates". Even more famous is
the mathematician Pythagoras, whose $a^2 + b^2 = c^2$ was
no doubt as revolutionary in its day as Einstein's $E = mc^2$
is today. Pythagoras (6th century) was also a musician and
philosopher.

For the Roman Emperor Augustus, Samos was a place of
winter retreat, and he made the island a Free State. From
1204 onwards, Samos was successively under Venetian,
Frankish and Genoese domination. In 1453, it fell to the
Turkish powers (the "Grande Porte"). During the Wars
of Liberation from Turkey, in the early part of the 19th
century, Samos won a measure of independence under
eventual Turkish sovereignty. Up till its incorporation into
a unified Greece in 1912, the island was ruled by rich landed
proprietors styling themselves "the princes of Samos".

The present capital, Samos, dates back to 1832. It adjoins
the old town of Vathi, and a harbor area. Vathi has more
than 5,000 inhabitants and is the business and tourist
center of the island. It contains the Archaeological Museum,
behind the park by the Xenia Hotel. At the back of the
harbor Customs House is a Museum of Byzantine Art.

There are numerous good bathing beaches in this area.
Firstly, there is a regular beach resort, with cabins and
showers, close to the harbor buildings. Then there is a
very popular natural beach inside the bay, and finally,
about a mile away is Ghagou Beach, connected by a good
bus service.

There are numerous regular bus trips and excursions from
the capital. In particular, while you are in the area, it is
recommended that you should make the short journey
to Turkey. There are connections from Vathi or Pythagorion to Kusadasi on the Turkish coast— while, from there,
it is only about an hour to the remarkable fields of ruins
of Ephesus, the town which was so great a center in ancient
times.

Before embarking on such an excursion, however, be sure
to enquire of the harbor police if there are any inoculation
requirements of which you stand in urgent need. This may
well save you time and trouble when you seek to re-enter
Greece from Turkey. Do not be surprised by the disproportionately high cost of these excursions—this is due to
the fact that a frontier crossing is involved. One small

point. In the Turkish check-out hall you will find a small
duty-free shop, selling whisky, tobacco, etc.—all the things
one normally finds within airport facilities.

And two final points relevant to a trip into Turkey. Don't
be caught by the first taxi-driver who offers to take you to
Ephesus for some 25 dollars. There are more spacious taxis
available, whose drivers will do the job for little more than
the equivalent of a dollar or two a time. They are slightly
less comfortable, but perfectly reliable. Also, unless you
are a really hardened type, wear your oldest shoes. This is
because the place swarms with shoe-shine boys, who will
give you no peace until you have accepted their attentions.
But they ask only a few coppers, and the easiest way is to
take some small change with you, and give at least one of
them the pleasure of giving you the shine of your life.

To get back to Samos. Now Vathi is certainly not the only
place of interest to the tourist. About 6 miles to the west
is Kokalion, also with good accommodation and several first
class restaurants. Close by are three good shingle beaches:
ask particularly for Psamadou Beach. This town is also the
ideal center from which to start long or short rambles in
the wooded mountain areas.

Some 12-13 miles west of Vathi are the charming villages
of Vourliotes and Aghios Konstantinos. About 6 miles
farther, and one comes into Karlovassion, the second largest
port on the island, conveniently divided into a new, middle
and old town. There are interesting bridges, fountains and
houses in the older parts, with a beautiful church and hotels
in the Palaeon quarter. There are good places for a swim
to the north and also south of the harbor: especially note-
worthy is the beach on the Gulf of Potamos, with a number of *taverna* restaurants and coffee shops. A curative
spring was discovered recently in the vicinity, and this is
bound to be placed under control and exploited in the near
future.

No tourist should leave Samos without visiting Pythagorion,
the enchanting little fisher port some 9 miles south of
Vathi. Its circular harbor dates back to antiquity. The
island capital was once located here, and the skilfully laid
4th century city wall is still preserved (originally some
4 miles in length). There are also the remains of a theater,
with a magnificent view over the sea below. Directly under
this spot is the opening of the famous Tunnel, and nearby
the Harbor Mole and remains of the Great Temple of Hera—
all of them wonders of ancient Samos and the work of the

great engineer-cum-architect Eupalinos, who worked for the tyrannical ruler Polycrates.

This ruler determined to ensure the city had a water supply which would be safe from enemies, so instructed Eupalinos to tunnel through Mount Ampelos above the town. The tunnel was about a kilometer long and was started from both ends. With an accuracy that was amazing for such primitive times, the two galleries proved to be about 6 feet out in the horizontal and some 9 feet out in the vertical plane, as they approached the meeting point. So a curve was made in the construction of each gallery, to ensure their perfect fit. A stoneware pipe was laid through, to carry the water.

About three miles south-west of Pythagorion is the Hereion, the remains of the Temple of Hera, once the greatest temple in all Greece. Now only one pillar remains upright of those once composing this 354 feet by 171 feet structure. The history and fate of the great temple has never been fully explained, and it is possible that it was, in fact, never completed.

All three of these remarkable works by Eupalinos were considered to be among the greatest engineering and structural feats of the ancient Greek world. In addition, the Temple of Hera is considered one of the Seven Great Wonders of Antiquity.

A Diversion to Ikaria

About 11 miles west of Samos lies Ikaria, a scenically attractive little island which is mainly touched by ships running from Piraeus to the Asia Minor islands. It covers about 100 square miles and has a population around 1,000. The capital, Aghios Kirikos, lies in the south-east, and close by are the sulphur baths at Therma, a popular Greek resort.

The island owes its name to Icarus, a figure from mythology. He was the son of Daedalus, a great artificer, who was able to fly by means of a pair of specially constructed wings fastened to his back. On one occasion Icarus used these, against his father's advice. He flew too close to the sun, so that the wax fastening the wings melted, and Icarus plunged to his doom.

Chapter Seven

THE CYCLADES

There are over 200 islands in this group, in the heart of the Aegean Sea. But only about 20 of the islands are above 4 square miles in area. Typical of the Cyclades are the cube-shaped, whitewashed and flat-roofed houses, ornamented dovecotes, churches with blue-tinted domes, windmills, and the celebrated brilliant light of the area. At the center of the group lies Delos, one of the greatest shrines of antiquity.

Kea—A Romantic Introduction to the Group

Kea (area 50 square miles; population 2,000) is often still popularly known as Tzia, and is the largest of the western islands of the group. There are said to be some 200 churches on the island. . . .

In the Turkish Crusade the island fell to four Venetian knights, who divided it between them. In the 16th century it came under the Dukedom of Naxos and was occupied by the Turks in 1566. Sites of a number of ancient towns may be found here. Near to the present capital, Kea, is the site

of ancient Joulis. The present town is on a height behind
powerful fortifications. For centuries this was the only
settlement on the island, where the inhabitants huddled
together for protection against marauding pirates. Don't
miss the archaic lions hewn out of the rock, about a mile
north of the town.

In antiquity, the source of the island's prosperity was its
mineral wealth—today it is its fine sandy beaches. These
are, especially, at Kortissa (also called Livadi) and Vour-
kari. They offer peace and quiet, a certain seclusion, in
unsophisticated surroundings.

Siros—A One-Time Shipping Terminus

Siros (area 320 square miles; population 20,000) may also
be termed Syra or Syros. The lengthy docking procedures
at this island—the endless, and seemingly pointless lying at
anchor, before being allowed to disembark—seem calculated
to put one off at the outset.

But if this is lost time for the traveler, it certainly is not for
the locals, who swarm over the ship selling Turkish honey
(*loukoumia*) and nougat, for which Siros is noted throughout the Aegean. If you are not calorie-conscious, make the
most of these delicacies. The matronly shape of most of
the older Greek women here is sufficient indication of the
effects of indulgence!

Siros's special advantage would appear to be its central
position—yet it seems to have been of little significance
in antiquity. Only at Chalandriani in the north-east have
any remains been found of an ancient settlement. The
island is praised in Homer for its good pasturage, wine
and wheat.

Siros achieved little importance until the 19th century,
when it remained neutral during the Greek Wars of Liberation. In the Middle Ages it was under Venetian influence
and for a long time belonged to the Dukedom of Naxos.
In the 13th century the Venetians founded the city of
Anosyros—today standing on the higher of the two hills
overlooking the present capital, Hermoupolis. Anosyros
became the chief town of the island and was the seat of
a Roman Catholic Bishop. A majority of the population
converted to the new faith, several monasteries were
founded, and a delegation of Capuchins in Paris drew
Louis XIII's especial attention to Siros. This had for-
tunate consequences. After the occupation of Siros by

the Turks in 1566, the good relations between France and the "Grande Porte" guaranteed the freedom of worship to the non-Orthodox Catholics. It was also for this reason that the Siriots took a neutral stance in the Wars of Liberation from the Turks, and were spared the horrible massacres that occurred on nearby Chios and Psara in 1822.

Many fugitives from the Chios massacre fled to Siros and founded a new city on Vrontado, the neighboring hill to Anosyros. Eventually, the newcomers built the present city of Hermoupolis (Greek: Ermoupolis) on the shores of the bay below. The name derives from Hermes, the Greek god who, among other things, was "responsible" for commerce. Within a few years, the port became the central harbor for all Greece. But this development had come to an end by the last years of the nineteenth century, by which time Piraeus had taken the lead as the main shipping terminal.

Today the capital, with 14,000 inhabitants, is an administrative seat, while its harbor is still of importance as the loading point for the agricultural products of the Cyclades. It is also still a meeting-point for numerous shipping lines traveling between Piraeus and the islands of the group. The times when Siros was a favorite Greek holiday haunt are long since past—nevertheless, it can still offer good accommodation and relaxation.

Hermoupolis itself has many good hotels. If you decide to spend a few days here, above all visit St. George's Cathedral in Anosyros, also the city hall and nearby church of Aghios Nikolaos, in the center of the town. The most popular resort on the island is Possidonia, also known as Della Grazia, in the south-west. Here there are some good hotels and fine, sandy beaches. The fishing harbor, with its *tavernas*, has particular charm. From here, you can conveniently make excursions to neighboring beaches or islands.

Kithnos—The Mule-Breeders' Island

Kithnos (area 39 square miles; population 2,000), the southerly neighbor of Kea, is popularly known as Thermia. It is generally somewhat drier than Kea, and consequently less fertile; for a long time its prosperity came from the import and breeding of mules. Shipping anchors off the Bay of Aghia Irini on the north-east tip and close to the bathing resort of Loutra, held in high esteem since antiquity. Bathing facilities are unsophisticated, but there is plenty of evidence of the curative effect of the two old

springs here, especially in cases of rheumatism. The waters
are said to contain bromine, iodine, phosphorus, carbonate
of lime, sulphur, and arsenates.

About 4 miles south of this spot is the island's *chora* or
capital, also called Kithnos. Just over a mile from the sea, it
has about 900 inhabitants and close by, some caves with
stalactites and stalagmites. Some 4 miles farther south is
Driopis, a township surrounded by windmills. North-west
from here, at Evraikastro, are the ruins of ancient Kithnos.
Near the north cape of the island are the ruins of the medieval settlement of Oriastro Kastro.

Prices on Kithnos are relatively low, but there are clean
hotels and plenty of unspoiled *tavernas*. But getting there
isn't all that easy. Sometimes you will have to wait a few
days in Athens for a ship that is making a call at Irini Bay.

Serifos—Island of Iron

Serifos (area 28 square miles; population 1,800) lies about
11 miles south of Kithnos and 8 miles south-east of Sifnos.
This is a place to which to withdraw from the madding
crowd for a brief period. The island is almost round, except
for the deep bite taken by the unbelievably blue water of
Livadion Bay in the south-east corner. The township here
has achieved importance as the loading point for ores mined
on the island. Serifos has been known since antiquity for
copper and lead—though today, it is mainly from iron that
the island's income derives.

There are fine beaches and a category B hotel in Livadion.
The capital, Serifos, lies high above the harbor. It has some
800 inhabitants and displays the line of windmills and Venetian fort which are so typical of the Cyclades. A "must"
for all visitors is a trip to the Taxiarchos monastery, just
3 hours from Livadion: it has enchanting 18th century
frescoes and a collection of beautiful manuscripts.

Sifnos—Once Rich in Gold and Silver

Sifnos (area 28 square miles; population 2,300) has a
fertile eastern side and even produces some wine. Ships
anchor off Kamares on the west coast, and passengers go
ashore in small boats. A bus connects the harbor with
the capital, Apolonia, and its neighbor, the village of
Artemon. Kastro, the medieval capital, is built into the
side of a hill and surrounded by a powerful wall. It was

built on the site of the ancient island center, which owed its prosperity to the presence here of gold and silver.

Several of the ancient mines may be found at Aghios Suzon, on the east coast, though most of the galleries are now under water. Remains of ancient mines will also be found at Aghia Mina and Kapsalos, and on the northern slopes of Mount Profitis Elias. Kamares, the anchorage bay, is today renowned for its pottery and ceramic work.

Milos—Best-Known of the Islands

Milos (area 58 square miles; population 5,000) is known throughout the world on account of the famous statue of Aphrodite, the "Venus de Milo", which was unearthed here in 1822. Today, the original graces the Louvre in Paris, while the unfortunate islanders have only a plaster copy in the museum in the capital, Plaka. There have always been rumors that the original statue was found complete, and the arms were destroyed during the course of the bitter wrangles which understandably surrounded its removal to France.

There is little habitation in the western part of the island, dominated by the peak of Mount Profitis Elias (2,400 feet). Milos is almost cut in half by the deep bay which bites into the northern coast. There is every evidence this marks the crater of a volcano which destroyed itself in a violent eruption. In many parts of the island the original rock base is covered by volcanic material—especially pumice stone, quartz and lava. This would also account for the presence of obsidian, a quick-cooling, very hard lava mass, which was used from neolithic times onwards for shaping and cutting tools, particularly for knives and spear heads. This brought Milos fame in antiquity: the great sculptor Phidias is said to have worked with tools from Milos obsidian.

The ancients also praised Milos for other natural resources—alum, pumice, kaolin and sulphur particularly. During the Middle Ages, Milos belonged, most of the time, to Venice.

The harbor of Adamas has some small hotels and excellent beaches. From here you can travel by boat to Aghios Demitrios, a good center for rambles. Mount Profitis Elias is best climbed starting from the harbor of Ravari, in the south. The climb takes 3 hours, passing a beautiful Chapel of Mary.

Going south from Adamos, you reach the beach of Chiva-dolimni: close by is a small lake. Farther west, there is a good bathing beach at Brovatas Bay. Going north-west from Adamos, you reach Plaka (or Milos), the capital, in about 2 miles, by way of the village of Tripiti. The capital has some 1,000 inhabitants. Apart from the museum, there are nearby excavations, where you will find the remains of a Temple to Dionysus and a school. On the way to Tripiti are early Christian catacombs, containing some 2,000 bodies in their niches.

Further good beaches are at Apolonia (north-east) and Vodias (east coast). An unforgettable memory will be a boat tour of the island, and possibly visits to the neighboring islets of Kimolos, Antimilos and Poliegos. They form a geological unity with Milos. One thing, however, to remember. If you feel you just *can't* do without your own private shower and toilet adjoining your bedroom, you're likely to find difficulty with accommodation on Milos!

Andros

Andros (area 147 square miles; population 12,000) is separated from the mainland of Euboea by a 7-1/2 mile wide channel, called by Venetians the Canal d'Oro. The island, which is the most northerly of the Cyclades, and the second largest (after Naxos), can be reached during the summer months by steamer from Piraeus. This is by a line which sails once a week, calling at Kea, Andros, Siros and Kithnos. However, the crossing is somewhat notorious, for the sea can be very rough in this area at the height of summer. A much quicker route is by way of Rafina on the eastern shores of Attica, connected by a feeder bus service to Athens. This is a daily ferry-and-bus service.

Capital of the island is Andros (population 2,000), lying on a high ridge between two fertile valleys. The remains of the medieval fortress are still to be seen on the forward slopes. Worth seeing in the town are the church of Svododios Pigi, with a carved iconostasis dating from 1717; and the 15th century Roman Catholic church of Andreas.

Among excursions which can be made from Andros town there is a delightful walk to Apikia, the source of the mineral water "Sarisa", known throughout Greece. Southeast of the town, the Bay of Korthion bites into the island. Korthion is a tiny village in fertile countryside, with a category C hotel of good reputation.

The most important villages on the western coast of the
island are Gavrion and Batsion. The latter has become a
tourist center and has the largest choice of hotels. About
5 miles south of Batsion are the remains of the ancient
capital of Palaeopolis, close to a fishing village which still
bears the name. But there are no very extensive remains
to be seen—mainly some fragments of the ancient harbor
mole and the city wall. Some ceramics and statuary have
been removed to the museum in the new capital. The
finest relic, the "Hermes of Andros", has been removed to
the National Museum in Athens.

The 3,000 feet high Mount Kuvari towers over Palaeopolis.
It is best climbed from Batsion via the village of Pitiofos,
whence it is three hours to the top, and the reward of a
magnificent view!

Tinos—Island of the Miraculous Image

Tinos (area 77 square miles; population 9,000) in the
eastern Cyclades, is especially renowned for its possession
of the "Panaghia Evangelistra", also known as the "Christo-
spiliopsia", an icon of the Virgin Mary, to which miraculous
healing powers are ascribed. It forms the centerpiece of a
church which is an object of pilgrimage for tens of thousands
of people from throughout Greece on the great feasts of
Mary, especially those of March 25th and August 15th each
year. Difficulties in finding accommodation have so far
hindered the writer from staying in Tinos on one of these
special days. But the attraction of the image draws pilgrims throughout the year, and at other times I have
watched with awed amazement as the injured and crippled
hobble to the shrine. Among these are some of the poorest
of the poor, whose entire livelihood may depend on the
generosity of other pilgrims. . . .

Inside, the shrine is an orgy of pictures, candles and incense.
On the ground floor, the spot is marked where a nun, in the
last century, found the picture, after it had been indicated
to her in a dream. There are also two baptistries, where
daily baptisms are carried out before animated crowds.
Unlike the Roman Catholic, the Greek Orthodox priest
still practices baptism by full immersion. Around the
church are grouped four buildings in which believers wait
fervently for healing. I have to admit that after a splendid
meal, and a good deal of *retsina* straight from the barrel, I
was so tired I simply stretched out full length in one of
these rooms to rest. But it helped make my experience of
this island unforgettable. . . .

If you come to Tinos outside the times of major pilgrimage, you will find it offers all the amenities of any island in the Cyclades. In and around the capital, Tinos, there are numerous good hotels and plenty of private accommodation. You will find simple guest facilities in the pretty little villages throughout the island, and plenty of peace and quiet.

There are plenty of good bathing beaches. Specially recommended are the following: along Aghios Joannis Bay in the south-west some 4-1/2 miles from the capital; at Aghios Fokas, on the west coast, served by regular bus services; at Monia, 2-1/2 miles north-west of Tinos town, reached by bus or boat.

Some years ago, the remains of an ancient temple of Poseidon were unearthed, near Kionia. The sea-god was particularly venerated here in antiquity, as he is said to have rid the island of a plague of snakes. Poseidon's remedy was simple. He imported one or two storks, which very quickly exterminated the pests.

A number of pleasant excursions can be made from Tinos. In particular, to the 1,600 feet high Mount Exoborgo, once the site of the fortresses of the Venetian masters of Tinos and neighboring Mykonos. Numerous Turkish attacks were repulsed, so that the two islands remained an outpost of the Venetian Republic till 1718. A worthwhile trip can be made to the village of Chinara, about 9 miles from Tinos town. The residence and cathedral of a Roman Catholic Bishop are located here. And on the way back, don't fail to visit the Convent of Kechrovunion, dating from the 12th century. Here, you will be shown the cell of Sister Pelagia, the nun to whom the hiding place of the wonder-working icon was revealed.

The Brilliance of Mykonos

In his excellent book on the Greek Islands ("The Companion Guide", published by Collins in the U.K.), Ernle Bradford has this to say of Mykonos (area 34 square miles; population 3,700): "It is the most whitewashed town in all the islands, and the glare and razzle-dazzle of the streets is almost blinding. Dark glasses are no affectation here. . . . "

This is certainly no exaggeration. But the fact is that the popularity of Mykonos among central European holiday-makers has also led to some exaggerated and distorted

accounts which present a quite false picture of the island.
It is described as the island which has everything—the atmosphere of the Cyclades, all tourist amenities, churches,
windmills and night-clubs, etc., etc. Let's look at each of
these in turn.

The atmosphere of the Cyclades: Well, this exists equally
on all the other islands of the group. The only difference
is that, on Mykonos, only too many of the beautiful homes
of ordinary citizens and craftsmen have been turned into
night clubs and souvenir shops.

All tourist amenities: Of itself, this is no special advantage—
in fact, the notoriety gained by Mykonos has led, if anything, to too much exploitation.

The churches: Now, in one sense, these really are remarkable. There are said to be some 365 churches amid the
maze of streets—one for each day of the year. But unless
you have an obsession for churches, only one is really of
interest—that of Paraportiani (which means "before the
gates"). This lies on the west bank of Mykonos town and
shelters some seven chapels under one intricate roof. In
the same area you will find those houses with decorated
balconies which have given the town the name of "Little
Venice".

Windmills on Mykonos are just like those on the other
islands—except that they're photographed more! In general,
they have only a nostalgic value, corn being today almost
universally ground by electric power.

The night clubs: Certainly, there are more of these on
Mykonos than on all the other islands put together. The
dolce vita of Mykonos is a byword, but the artists who
originally "discovered" the island are no longer prominent
there. One sees some way-out types, some eccentrics, some
homosexual couples (male and female) and so on. But to
come to Mykonos simply to make that sort of contact
would be a mistake.

But the island is beautiful, perhaps too beautiful! Up till
now there has been a handful of hotels where the visitor
gets top treatment—either on a beach, or with the bus
or boat stop for the beach just outside the door. The most
popular beaches are in the south: Aghios Joannes, Platis
Giolos, and three known as Paradise, Super-Paradise and
Hell (this latter is named after the Greek word for olive
trees, *elia*).

To reach the beaches, you either take the bus (the stop is
behind the Olympic Airways Office), or a boat round the
western cape of the island. When the sea is too rough, it
may be better to go on foot, male-female couples preferring
Paradise Beach, while the male-male and female-female

couples seem to prefer Super-Paradise. The author must admit he's never yet ventured into Hell. The road back from Super-Paradise is very varied and beautiful, if you decide to return on foot. As to nude bathing, this is silently tolerated on Mykonos—though, as elsewhere in Greece, it is officially forbidden.

One thing you will certainly see in **Mykonos harbor is Petros** the pelican. He is said to have alighted on the island some years ago in an exhausted condition. An islander cared for him, he stayed, and has become a sort of island mascot. You'll generally find him near Aghios Nikolaos Church. . . .

Delos—Hub of the Cyclades

Delos (area 1.35 square miles; permanent population 1) is dominated—if that is the right word—by the 360 feet high peak of Mount Kinthos, its outstanding geographical feature.

The island can be reached by boat from either Mykonos, Paros or Naxos—seas permitting. But even when the seas permit, this is not to say you won't need your sea-sickness tablets! The Aegean can be very rough in this quarter.

It is when you ascend this island peak that you see clearly, perhaps for the first time, why Delos is so often referred to as the hub of the Cyclades. The first settlements here were in some 3,000 B.C., but it was not till around 1,000 B.C. that, owing to this commanding position, Delos became the religious center of the Ionian masters of Greece. According to legend, both Apollo and his twin sister Artemis were born on the island. Through the 7th, 6th and 5th centuries B.C., Delos remained a cultural and financial center of the Greek world. But in 454 B.C. the island treasury was removed to safer keeping in the Parthenon of Athens, and from that moment the significance of Delos declined.

In the 3rd century B.C. Delos again assumed importance, under Egyptian protection—and, with the help of Greek rulers, many new buildings were added. Finally, under Roman rule, from about 150 B.C. on, the island found, for a time, continuous prosperity as a merchant shipping and banking center. For Delos lies smack in the center of two great ancient sailing routes—from Crete to the entrance to the Black Sea, and from the last mainland of Europe (in Greece) to the first mainland of Asia (in present-day Turkey). Added to which, it is a naturally sheltered harbor.

Although the only permanent inhabitant of Delos is the keeper of the museum, there is a small tourist hostel, if you wish to stay overnight. Apart from the famous terrace of the lions, the greatest sights in Delos are in the former commercial city. Look at the Temple of Apollo, the Sanctuary of Artemis, the Sanctuary of the Bulls, the *Agora* (market place), the porticos of Philip and Antigone, the Museum, the houses of Cleopatra, Dionysus, etc. Best of all, stay overnight, and in the evening, when the last boatload of tourists has left, this ancient center of religion, art and commerce will begin to exercise its real enchantment.

Paros—Home of the World's Finest Marble

Paros (area 75 square miles; population 8,000) was celebrated in antiquity for the quality of its marble. Of the various types found on the island, the most famous was *Lychnites*, named after *lychnos* meaning candle-light, because it was by this light that the precious stone was mined. It was said to be cleaner and more transparent than any other known sort. Leading workshops throughout the ancient world sought for this variety—including the schools of sculpture established on the island itself, which became celebrated in the 6th and 5th centuries B.C.

Parian marble was famed right into Roman times. In fact, today, in the Caracalla Thermae in Rome, you can see engraved on a block the name of the Roman foreman-supervisor, and the exact origin of the block in Paros. Two of the ancient mines are still open and can be visited. You will need strong shoes and a guide with flashlamps. The mine is reached from Parikia, after about 3-3/4 miles on the Lefkes-Marpissa-Drios bus route. On leaving the bus, climb slightly about 250 yards in a southerly direction, and the mine lies in a depression on the left.

But there is also much else of interest on this island. Your boat arrives at the capital, Parikia, also known as Paros, on an elongated west coast bay. To the north-east is Naoussa, a little fishing town with a unique harbor, entirely bordered by marble slabs, and a great tourist attraction.

At present, the general direct approach to Paros is by steamer from Piraeus, a voyage of about 8 hours, and often stormy in late summer. But an airport in the neighboring island of Naxos is due for completion in 1975, and visitors to Paros will then no doubt fly to Naxos and transfer the

by local boat. The Parian port for inter-
...ffic is Naoussa, which has a regular bus connec-
...(every 30 minutes) with the capital. From Naoussa a
caïque travels daily to Delos and Mykonos, returning each
evening. But like the Mykonos-Delos connection, this
route is also dependent on the weather. And if the captain
of the boat you hoped to travel on decides against making
the trip, please don't try to dissuade him. Long years of
experience have taught him that what seems like an insigni-
ficant breeze to you, may well be a prelude to the sort of
storm that blows up in this area.

Naoussa is the second largest town on the island. It has
some hotels and some excellent private accommodation.
Above all, for families with small children, there is a
splendid holiday home. The narrow streets cannot be
negotiated by vehicles. Good beaches can be easily reached,
the best of them by motor-boat.

Naoussa's square harbor is among the most delightful I
know. I once spent an entire day in the little coffee-shop
(*kafenion*) in the farthest corner. Starting with a breakfast
of curds and honey, I watched the fishermen unloading
and preparing their fish, then about mid-day witnessed a
great coming and going of *caïques*, followed by a siesta,
when the local folk exchanged the latest small town gossip.
Finally, as dusk fell, I dined superbly on octopus.

Wherever you go on the islands, you will find, as I did then,
that local people have an entirely different conception of
time from their counterparts in more northern latitudes.
Leisure time—the time when you don't *have* to work—is
regarded as one of the priceless treasures of life, to be
whiled away securely in small talk that has probably
changed little in two or three thousand years.

But to get back to the capital, which—as we have seen—has
two names, a practice very common in the Aegean. Parikia
or Paros (more often found on Greek maps), has 2,000
inhabitants, and lies on a deep, protected bay, so that
even large ships can dock there. Right on the quay is a
windmill, in which the Greek Tourist Police have an office.
A large notice, in English, points out that all nude bathing
is forbidden.

A few hundred yards west of the harbor mole is one of the
most beautiful churches in the Aegean (many claim, *the*
most beautiful). This is Ekatontapiliani (the church of a
hundred gates). Dating partly back to the 5th century, it
has recently been extensively restored, and is one of the

oldest examples of early Catholic churches. It is, in fact, three churches in one. The earliest part is the small basilica of Saint Nicholas; centrally, is the great cruciform main church; to the south is the baptistry. The apse contains seats for the clergy, with a central throne for the bishop. The church is more commonly known as the Katapoliani (meaning low (or lower) down).

Other ancient sites in Parikia are not so easy to find—but at least walk the few steps from the Katapoliani to the museum. Among other relics here, there is a piece of the so-called Parian marble, and a copy of an ancient chronicle, carved in marble and containing the birth date of Homer. The center of the capital is that of a typical Cyclades town, with much charm. There are numberless boutiques, and shops selling art and craft work, especially knitted wear (you can have a garment knitted to measure here!), also enameled and gold and silver jewellery. A very special souvenir is a small mussel shell set in gold, and said to bring the purchaser life-long good luck. Dolo Roberts, a woman painter from Germany who has lived many years on Paros, has a workshop in the town and sells some delightful oil paintings.

Many pleasant trips can be made, using Parikia as a center. Above all, on the Lefkes-Marpissa-Drios bus mentioned above—which, apart from passing the old quarries described, stops at a fine beach on the east coast, where there is also a variety of accommodation. Roughly central to the island is the peak of Mount Profitis Elias (2,300 feet), which is best climbed from Parikia by way of the village of Kalogeria, and the convent of Christos ton Dasus. Another spot to visit is Petaloudes, where there is a "butterfly vale", similar to that on Rhodes, where clouds of butterflies swarm. It is best reached on mule or donkey.

While in the area, the island enthusiast will not want to miss a visit to Antiparos, the neighboring isle to the south-west (area 13 square miles; population 500). Best reached by boat from Parikia, Antiparos has some fantastic beaches by Kastro in the south-east, and also some fine caves with stalactites and stalagmites. Most to be admired, perhaps, is the simple life that folk here are still able to lead.

Naxos—Lord Byron's Dream Isle

Naxos (area 166 square miles; population 16,000) was praised by Byron as a dream island, and only his premature death frustrated his plan to retire here. Byron first visited the island in 1810—but it has had a good image right from antiquity. Naxos figures in a number of Greek myths. In particular, it was said to be the island to which Theseus, the legendary hero from Attica, brought Ariadne, after he had abducted her from Crete. Once here, Theseus cheerfully overlooked his promises of marriage and sailed home to Attica and the eventual throne of Athens. The abandoned Ariadne then took up with Dionysus, the god of wine, who made her his wife, and—in a beautiful legend—placed among the stars the crown he gave her at their marriage. This now appears in the heavens as the constellation Corona Borealis, an almost perfect semi-circle of stars between Boötes and Hercules.

Though the legendary couple, at their wedding feast, no doubt drank Naxos wine, which was celebrated in ancient Greece, today the toasts on Naxos are more likely to be drunk in *kitron*. This is a liquor made from a secret blend of the fruit and leaves of citrus trees. A bottle makes an ideal souvenir to take back from your holiday.

The island has always stood in a sort of special light. Herodotus, the ancient Greek historian, described it as being richer than all the other islands in simple "happiness". It is constantly impressive—but perhaps the most powerful impression you will get of the island is that when you first arrive. After your steamer has cruised down the channel between Paros and Naxos you face the range of mountains which extends the whole length of the island, with the hill on which the capital is built rising in front. As the ship gets nearer, you will see to the left of the harbor entrance a high ridge topped by a tall arch composed of three mighty slabs of white marble. These are the preserved remains of a 600 B.C. Temple of Apollo. The temple was never completed, but its foundations show it would have become one of the greatest centers of homage to the gods in all antiquity. In 500 A.D. an early Christian basilica was built on the same spot—but of this, too, only the portal remains.

Naxos is the largest of the Cyclades islands, with a mountain chain that rises to over 3,000 feet and is partly responsible for the pleasant climate. Island products are varied—from citrus fruits and olives to every other kind of fruit and vegetable, such as artichokes, early tomatoes, figs, almonds and potatoes. Wheat, too, is cultivated here. For Naxos has a plentiful supply of that invaluable commodity that is comparatively rare in the Cyclades—water. This is distributed by an agricultural union in accordance with ancient laws and rights.

Of the population, some 2,500 live in the *chora*, or capital, which is also called Naxos. This is also the tourist center of the island, albeit the beach is not an overwhelmingly attractive one. But from the capital there are a number of ways of reaching the fine beaches along the west coast—though whatever way you go, they are some 1—2 miles by foot or vehicle.

There has been a settlement on the city hill since ancient times. During the centuries of the ascendancy of Venice, the Venetian knight Sanudi built a fortress here, after he had secured ownership of the island in 1204. His influence was so powerful that he formed a Dukedom of Naxos, which—though it was still under eventual Venetian control— had some measure of independent status.

After the extinction of the Sanudi family, the island passed into possession of the Carceri, then the Crispi family, which held the island till the mid-16th century against all the attacks from the Turks and from pirate marauders. Oddly enough, even after the general Turkish ascendancy, *this* island remained largely under Venetian control till it was handed over to the United Greece in 1830. The Venetian lords lived in the Palazzi, still preserved in the upper town. They kept their Roman Catholic faith, and today Naxos town has a resident Roman Catholic Archbishop as well as a school run by Ursuline nuns, attended by well-off young ladies from throughout Greece. Near to the Venetian fort is an interesting small museum.

The lower town, with its closely-packed, cubic white houses, presents the usual Mediterranean picture. By the harbor there are numerous *tavernas* and coffee shops, and a few small stores.

South of the capital, a modern tourist center is springing up at Alyko-Pyrgaki: it can be reached by bus, over a good road. Here, a complete holiday resort is growing, with colonies of leisure bungalows and a hotel with 750 beds. Though many of those who had previously enjoyed a taste of the simple life on Naxos may regret such an appearance, it must be admitted that preparations have to be made for the airport which is to operate here from 1975 on.

One bonus brought to the island by its abundance of water is the great wealth of flowers. Especially, everywhere by the water-courses, you will find luxuriant growths of blossoming oleander trees.

The most popular excursion spot on the island is the little
harbor village of Aghios Joannes, at the northern end of
the east coast, and some 26 miles from the capital. It can
be reached by bus, more expensively by taxi, best of all
by motor boat round the north cape of Naxos. Above the
picturesque group of houses is an ancient quarry, called
Ston Apollona, which has become an alternative name
for the settlement. Here there lies a huge statue, over 30
feet long, which had evidently been cut from the quarry
and immediately worked upon. But it's clear that the
sculptors found faults in the material, especially in the
head area, and abandoned their task. Although it's not
certain the statue was meant to be of Apollo, this is the
generally accepted construction. The beard, however,
suggests it might have been intended as Dionysus.

Between the villages of Melanes and Potamia you will find
further uncompleted statues in ancient marble quarries.
There is also a 20 feet long block apparently intended for
the city's temple arch, but abandoned because of faults in
the marble.

Naxos abounds in finds for arts enthusiasts: it is like a
large museum of Byzantine architecture and painting.
Here are some high spots for the student of painting:

— at Sangri, south-east of the capital, the Church of Aghios
Nikolaos, with the fine late 13th century frescoes; also the
9th century Church of Aghios Artemios;

— farther east, in the center of the island, the fertile Tragea
Valley, with its delightful villages;

— in Chalki, the Church of Protothoroni has fine 10th
century frescoes in the dome. While in Chalki don't fail
to enquire for the nearby Church of Aghios Giorgos
Diasoritis: it has 11th century frescoes which include a
charming nativity scene, and a splendid scene of the Last
Judgment in the porch area;

— at Kaloxylo, near Chalki, the Church of Paneghia
Damiotissa has unusual 13th century frescoes;

— at Moni, look at the Church of Paneghia Drosani;
again, it is the early frescoes which will fascinate students
of painting.

Architecturally, too, the island boasts some fascinating
objects, such as:

— high above the Apollonia quarry, the medieval fortress of Kalogero;

— in the Tragea Valley, numerous fortified towers, which were erected to serve as sanctuaries for noble families from Italy, when under attack;

— north of Chalki, in the exceptionally charming, high village of Apeirantos, some impressive old mansions. In the same spot, the Church of St. Kyriaki is of great interest, showing frescoes which scorn any reproduction of the human figure;

— an hour's travel from the capital, the Convent of Chriso-stomos;

— farther to the north-west, via the village of Engares, the Monastery of Vaneromeri.

One thing you will find for certain on this island—or, at least, until such time as it has been really opened up to the tourist industry—is a hospitality which has been a byword for centuries.

Santorin (or Thira)—and the Lost City of Atlantis

Mention Santorin, and a light appears in the eyes of any experienced Aegean traveler. It is a unique island, stranger than any other, even in the colorful world of the Greek Islands.

To begin with, it has, or has had, many names. Santorin, still commonest in English texts, is a corruption of the title given it by its medieval Venetian masters, who called the island after its patron saint, Irene. In antiquity, the isle was called Thera, apparently after the founder of a Doric city of that name. This is also the name you will now find on Greek maps and official literature, though it is spelt Thira. The Greeks themselves only use Thira of the capital, and then it is generally pronounced Phira—a relic of the ages of domination by the Turks, who could not get their tongue round the "th".

The history of the island is as full of variety as its termi-nology. For it is clear that the sickle-shaped piece of land once formed a full circle, joined to the neighboring islets of Thirassia and Aspronisi. This gave rise to another of its ancient names—Stronghili (the round). But the group lies on a geological fault, and its eventful history is a tale of continuous volcanic action. Earlier than 800,000 B.C. there was unbroken land between Greece and Asia Minor.

Following the break-up of this area into the Aegean and
its islands, all that existed of present-day Santorin was
the peak of the modern Mount Profitis Elias. Repeated
volcanic activity in the area gradually covered this peak
with ash and cinders, until an island had formed. As with
most volcanic rock, this proved very fertile, and the island
blossomed with rich vegetation. This accounts for yet
another of its ancient names—Kalliste (the fairest).

Some time after 2,000 B.C. there was a disaster of un-
paralleled magnitude in the area. To begin with, the
outlets of the old craters had long since been stopped up
with their old laval waste. As new pressures built up, the
gases and molten material were at first probably only able
to escape through fissures and cracks—but the resultant hail
of ash and brimstone was sufficient to destroy or drive out
all vegetation and living creatures. Finally, a gigantic explosion destroyed the entire crust of the land mass and
water rushed in to fill up the giant basin which replaced it.
During the course of time, further volcanic peaks have
thrust to the surface of this vast lagoon, and have formed
fresh islands. Two of these are called Nea Kameni and
Palea Kameni, the first being still an active cone, last
erupting in 1950.

Present-day archaeologists have linked this all-time catastrophe with the otherwise unexplained phenomenon of
the abrupt disappearance of the great Minoan civilization
on the island of Crete, also some time after 2,000 B.C. For
after a certain point in time, all the ancient palaces, the
fleet and all the panoply of this great culture have been
found destroyed. It is theorized that the Santorin explosion caused a giant tidal wave which could easily cover
the 70 odd miles to Crete, and wiped out entire cities there.
And what the tidal wave did not destroy would no doubt
have disappeared in subsequent earthquakes.

Archaeologists have found confirmation of this theory in
the effects of the Krakatoa disaster of the 1920s, when
the explosion of a volcano produced a tidal wave fifty
feet high, which wreaked enormous destruction on inhabited areas hundreds of miles distant.

A leading theorist in this connection is Greek archaeologist Professor Spiro Marinatos. In 1967 his views received
astonishing support from the discovery, beneath the village
of Akrotirion in southern Santorin, of an entire Minoan
city, complete with two- and three-storey buildings in
excellent preservation. The buildings have been painstakingly separated from the enveloping pumice stone, and

form an archaeological find of sensational importance. A visit to this area is essential to anyone with an interest in the ancient history of the area. Most of the buildings, with their decorations and frescoes are very well preserved, and a museum is to be built to house the countless treasures unearthed.

It is difficult to say just when the name of Santorin first became linked with that fabulous city of pre-history tantalisingly described by Plato in his "Timaeus"—the lost city of Atlantis. But in 1960, Angelos Galanopoulos, a Professor of Seismology, pointed out the remarkable concurrence between the known geological history of the Santorin archipelago and the descriptions given of Atlantis in the Platonic dialogues. Hitherto, writers and historians have sought an Atlantis west of Gibraltar, now they are again looking back to the area where the legend first grew.

Unfortunately, transport connections with Santorin are not as many as they might be. The former helicopter service from Athens has now been suspended. But several times a week a ship from Piraeus calls at Siros, Tinos, Mykonos and finally Santorin: a look at the map will show you this will hardly be a quick trip! Another way to get there is from Thessalonica, by way of a ship that does the Thessalonica-Skiathos-Skopelos-Skiros-Tinos-Mykonos-Santorin-Crete route twice a week. If you are already on another island fairly close, you will be able to book on a local *caïque*. According to the current (1974) timetable, the ship traveling from Crete north to Santorin arrives in the middle of the night. But don't let that put you off! The arrival of any ship is a real event for the local folk, and whatever hour it arrives, there will be plenty of people around. Also, don't expect island shipping *ever* to be strictly on time: it is almost always subject to delays.

But the right time to arrive at Santorin is unquestionably in daylight. Every travel writer describes with awed fascination his entry into the wide bay before the capital, with the brown-black cliffs, streaked with blood-red and electric green, rising sheer out of the water. Centrally are the smoking peaks of black islets which are still active volcanoes. It is unlike anything else in the Cyclades—or, in fact, anywhere. The ship anchors just off Thira, and passengers go ashore in small boats. By the beach are a few houses and coffee-shops.

The town of Thira stands atop the cliff, and a zig-zag path ascends for over a mile to get to it. Those with any kind

of disability or extra heavy packs, should ask the Tourist
Police for help. The town is 900 feet up, and there are
around 700 steps in the path leading to it. The usual
means of ascent is by hired mule or donkey, and I would
recommend you to enjoy this—not regard it as a sort of
purgatory. If your beast is too refractory, try saying a
few soothing words to it: the poor creatures are rarely
addressed with anything but harshness, and appreciate a
little encouragement for a change. And just occasionally
look down at the Aegean below, and up to the white
town.

When you arrive at the town, you will soon be aware of
the scars of the last earthquake to shake the area—on July
9th, 1956. Although the tremors lasted only a minute,
they left 50 dead, 200 injured, and more than 2,000
houses destroyed. Rehabilitation has been assisted by
Government subsidies, new more resistant houses of
concrete and steel have been erected—but nothing has
been able to restore the charm of the old town, as many
people living there will testify. At the same time, nothing
can change the grandeur of the view you still get over the
bay with its central Burnt Islands, as they are commonly
called.

The capital, which claims about 1,400 of the island population of 7,000, was founded in the early 16th century,
with a highly individualistic style of house—unfortunately,
scarcely detectable any longer, since the earthquake. There
are a number of hotels, and as you dismount from your
donkey you will find many local folk offering private
accommodation—most of it both clean and cheap. There
are a number of *tavernas*, some with balconies directly
over the drop to the gulf. It is delightful to sit here in the
evenings—but, more than elsewhere, you will need a woollen
jacket or sweater. Even in high summer, the height of the
town shows itself in the relative coolness of the air.

Thira town is a fine place for a shopping spree. Its unusual
situation gives your outing an added piquancy—and I am
constantly astonished at the immense variety of goods
obtainable—even on the most remote islands. It was in the
stores of Thira, too, that I first got an impression of the
fertility of this island, by the richness of the provender
available. Though, as you enter, you see only stark cliffs,
elsewhere there are gentle, green slopes.

In the east of the island is a regular anchorage, where ships
can land larger goods, even buses, etc., when the sea is

calm. All along this coast there are also fine beaches, though you must get used to one oddity—for here the sands vary from grey to black in color.

The best-known beaches on the island are at Monolithos, Kamari and Perissa, all of them along the lower half of the east coast (or outer edge of the crescent shape). At each beach, there are facilities for buying food and drink.

To return to the capital. In the northern part of the town, known as the Latin Quarter, there is a new museum, containing some remarkable exhibits—especially of finds from the excavations of the ancient capital town of Thera. Most of the excavation was carried out by a German archaeologist, Hiller von Görtringen, at his own expense. Görtringen died in 1947, but not before he had exposed much of the early history of the town.

It appears that after the giant catastrophe around 1,500 B.C., the first people to make any mark here were the Dorian Greeks, who, under the leadership of Thiras from Sparta, began to colonize the island from about 900 B.C. on. Gradually, order and prosperity were restored. The Dorians built their capital on Mezavuno, a spur of the peak of Mount Profitis Elias (1,800 feet), jutting into the sea. This spur is nearly 1,200 feet high, and is joined to the main peak by a saddle or col, called Sellada. It is only by way of this col that the ruins of the ancient town may be reached. In antiquity, this impregnable situation gave Thera, as the ancient capital was called, a position of great strength, and it played a key role in Aegean trading. The spur is flanked by good beaches, on which the flat-bottomed boats could be drawn up.

The three ways to reach these ruins are: by bus to Kamari, then on foot or by taxi to the col; by bus to Perissa, then on foot; from Pirgos (reached by bus), via the new road—which is O.K. for taxis—to the peak of Profitis Elias, then by foot some 300-400 yards over the col to ancient Thera.

The location of the town explains its elongated shape—some 800 yards long by a maximum of 150 yards wide. The eastern part shows the Dorian origins, but the residential part is more in a Hellenistic, i.e., late Greek and Roman, style. Water supply was mainly from cisterns, many of which have been dug up. The high degree of advancement of the inhabitants is shown, among other things, by the toilet and sanitary facilities which have been exposed.

As you enter the ruins by way of the Sellada, you first pass the Byzantine Church of St. Stephen, then, to the left, the path goes through a grotto to a kind of private shrine in honor of the Ptolemaic Admiral (Temenos des Artemidoros) of ancient Thera, from around 250 B.C. Following along this ancient Main Street, on the right you come to the command post and barracks of the Ptolemaic garrison, which occupied the town after the death of Alexander the Great. To the left was the Ptolemaic High School, of which some ruins remain. To the south-east lie the excavations of the residential area, with the remains of a theater, a temple to Dionysus and a Roman basilica, probably built under Augustus. Across from the theater, a house with a pillared courtyard and a temple to Apollo partly converted into a Byzantine church. Close by, a shrine to the Egyptian goddess, Isis.

The oldest remains are in the south-east corner of the rocky spur. Here there are signs of an archaic temple to Apollo Karneios, the Dorian family god, who was honored as lord of the island. Farther south-east, on the steep boundaries of the town, behind remains of some Roman baths, are the stones of another ancient High School. Everywhere, inscriptions are cut into the rock, and close by is the so-called Votive Rock, uncovered in 1835. It bears inscriptions which are quite clearly in praise of pretty boys and youths, cut by some older hand in an access of what our forbears chose to call "Greek love".

The excavations of the Minoan city near Akrotirion are reached by taxi, or in organized tours from the capital.

Those who have small interest in the ancient past can, of course, dispense with these outings—but, whatever else you do on Santorin, don't miss a trip to the top of the island's highest peak. As so often in the Greek Islands, it is called Mount Profitis Elias (the Prophet Elijah's Mountain), and the peak can be reached by taxi. It is not, of course, part of the volcano, but is the remaining chunk of the aboriginal landscape. At the top is a monastery, founded early in the 18th century, and still staffed by a few monks, who will welcome your visit. They have a large library, and a museum with ancient manuscripts, icons and silverware. Numerous other trips can be made from the capital. Some of these are as follows:

— By foot, to the north, via the district of Firostefani to Merovigli, passing an Orthodox convent. At Merovigli, the walls drop almost sheer to the sea, over 1,000 feet below.

A little lower down is the rocky area named Skaros, where the Venetians built a fortified capital.

— A little farther north (you will have to go on foot), the town of Ia or Oia. Like the capital, it stands high and is reached by a long zig-zag path from the beach.

— To the south of the capital, on the shore, lies Athinos, the town for the old harbor of Pyrgos. From here, a few years ago, a road was built to the higher areas of the island, so that now even handicapped people are able to visit Santorin. The road finishes just before Akrotirion, so can be used to get to the vicinity of the Minoan city excavations, and also to visit Balos, a tiny harbor village with a good beach.

— About an hour's walk to the west, you will reach the Akrotirion Cape lighthouse, where the geological enthusiast will find petrified remains of marine vegetation and creatures.

Caution. When wandering in the area of archaeological digs, take great care not to approach too closely to old washed-out excavations. The walls are often crumbly, and more than one person has stifled after tumbling into a mealy mass of brimstone sand.

However short a time you stay on Santorin, one excursion is essential—a trip to the active volcanic island in the bay. Two essentials for such a trip are: firstly, a calm sea, for it is difficult to land passengers in rough weather; secondly, a stout pair of shoes to deal with the laval fragments, which are often very sharp-edged. The ascent to the crater is relatively easy; higher up, you will see numerous escapes of steam and gas, a sure sign that the cone is still active. The higher temperature of the water round the island is also indicative of the volcano's life.

Another interesting, if somewhat less dramatic trip, is to the island of Thirassia, which, with the neighboring uninhabited Aspronisi constitutes all that remains above water level of the original lip of the crater. This trip is made from Thira town. On Thirassia a steep zig-zag path leads up to the main town, Manolas. There are two churches here, the larger being of most interest. As on Santorin, the dome is painted a pale blue to avoid dazzle. Grain, tomatoes and grapes are cultivated on the island, and locals claim that their wine is markedly better than that on the main island, though the writer must admit he found Santorin wine entirely palatable.

The Fringe Islands of the Cyclades

There are a number of small islands lying in the vicinity of
Santorin, which belong to the Greek administrative district
of Aparchia. All are fairly easily reached by *caïque* from
Thira town.

Amorgos (area 47 square miles; population 2,100) is an
elongated island, some 12 miles long and never much more
than 4 miles wide. The south-east coast is fairly straight
and steep, the north-west is more broken. In individual
bays lie two delightful harbors—Aegiali and Katapola. The
latter is considered the main one, and from it there are
occasional boat departures from Naxos, Ios and of course
Santorin. At Katapola the cliffs fall almost sheer into the
sea; behind them is the tranquil harbor, with a few arcades
and the remains of a Venetian fort on the quayside.

From the harbor there is a new road to the capital, Amorgos
(population 500), along which runs a bus service and even
taxis. When I first came here, the journey—which involves
climbing almost 1,000 feet—could only be made by mule.
The ruggedness of the countryside comes as a surprise after
the romantic little harbor. The little township is dominated
by a mighty fort, Apanokastro, built by the Genoese family
of Ghisi. When I was last there, the windmills round the
town were still in operation. They certainly never lacked
"puff", for the winds here seem to blow more strongly and
resolutely than anywhere else in the Aegean.

Especially worth visiting is the Monastery of Panaghia
Chozoviotissa, reached by mule from the capital in about
an hour. It was built in 1088, at the foot of a mighty
crag, and, in the words of Ernle Bradford, the writer already mentioned, "hangs in the sky like a wind-hovering
hawk". Center of the monastery is a miraculous picture
of the Madonna, which still draws pilgrims.

Two other trips, each of about 9-10 miles, can be made
from the capital. One is to the harbor township of Aegiali,
to the north-east; the other is to a fine, sandy beach near
the village of Kolofanou, to the south-west.

All in all, the seclusion of Amorgos means it is not everybody's cup of coffee, though its contrasting extremes of
rugged crags and fertile valleys make it one of the most
beautiful islands in the Aegean. There are some small
hotels in the harbor towns, and private accommodation.

Ios (area 42 square miles; population 1,400), known
locally as Nio, is the second largest island in this area.
Entrance is by way of a wide, fjord-like bay, leading to
the peaceful harbor of Ormos Nio. Round the harbor
square are coffee-shops and *tavernas*. There is plenty of
accommodation and there are some magnificent beaches.
Latterly, a number of bungalow hotels have been built in
the resorts, offering carefree holidays, especially for families with children.

A popular spot is Milokotos Bay to the south-east of the
harbor and easily reached: it has the best, and one of the
quietest beaches of the island. To the left of the harbor
entrance is the 18th century church of Aghia Irini, with
a striking dome and bell tower.

The capital, Ios (population 1,200) is about a quarter of
an hour from Ormos Nio harbor. Clean and inviting,
approached by way of terraced gardens with palm, pine
and eucalyptus trees, the capital is dominated by the 2,400
feet high peak of Mount Profitis Elias. On the north slope
of this mountain is an ancient burial place, said to contain
the bones of Homer. There is also a monastery, reached
in two hours on foot from Ios town.

This is a tranquil little island, and despite its rising popularity, it's to be hoped it will stay as it is—a peaceful paradise.

Sikinos (area 16 square miles; population 500), though
only separated from Ios by a 6 mile channel, presents a
complete contrast. To begin with, landing at Ormos Skala,
the island's only deep-water harbor, on Alopronia Bay, can
be almost impossible, even in good weather. Even so,
however, there are some delightful and quiet beaches along
the bay.

The main center of population on the island is Sikinos
town, reached in less than an hour, on foot or donkey, by
way of a mule-track, mostly through pleasant olive groves.
The township lies over the steep northern coast and a castle
dominates its center. In the south of the isle is the little
village of Vouni, and I've heard good reports that it is a
pleasurable walk from the "capital". The island is not
tourist-oriented, nevertheless you will always be sure of a
bed and food here.

Folegandros, the eastern neighbor of Sikinos, is an equally secluded isle. You land at Karavostasis on the north-east flank, then take the mule-path to the capital, Vathy—about an hour's journey. The capital stands on cliffs falling sheer into the sea, and has the remains of a Frankish castle. Though somewhat barren at first appearance, in fact this island has numerous springs in the valleys, and grain and beans are grown in the terraced fields.

Anafi, to the west of Santorin, is the last of its encircling islands. Measuring only about 11 square miles, the island is occasionally visited by ships from Kamari (on the east coast of Santorin). Again, landing is difficult, and this island really only recommends itself for longer stays, where the visitor wants to withdraw from the world for a time. I met a South African once who told me he had spent an entire summer on this little spot of land, without electric light, without piped water, washing in a spring at dawn, and going to bed along with the hens.

Strangely, in Athens, on the north slope of the Acropolis, there is an area known as the "Anafiotes' quarter". Its Cycladic aspect is the work of masons from this island who worked there as "immigrant labor" in the 19th century. By evening, it is one of the quietest and most charming parts of the Greek capital.

Chapter Eight

THE DODECANESE ISLANDS

The string of islands along the south-west coast of Turkey, with Rhodes as their center, have only been known as the Dodecanese since the beginning of this century. In antiquity and medieval times, the name Dodecanese (meaning twelve in Greek), had been applied to a group in the Cyclades, while the group around Rhodes was generally known as the Southern Sporades (Sporades meaning scattered or sprinkled).

Geologists ascribe the emergence of the Dodecanese (and related groups) to powerful earthquakes—deep in pre-history—which created some of the islands by breaking them away from the Asia Minor mainland, and others, by thrusting them up from the sea bed. Further theories suggest the land pattern was subject to constant change—the islands sometimes sinking again, and being over-run by the sea, as fossilized remains found in high mountain areas indicate. This submersion also smoothed out rugged rock formations, so that the Dodecanese today have relatively gentle coastlines.

From 1522 on, when Rhodes was conquered, the island group belonged to Turkey. Early in this century, separatist movements began to use the name Dodecanese to express unity among the group striving to achieve union with Greece. In 1912, with the help of Italian troops, the group broke the Turkish dominion—but the price they had to pay was renewed subjection—this time to Italy, with expansionist dreams of making the Mediterranean an Italian sea (*mare nostra*).

But if the Italians entirely ignored the islanders' pleas for union with Greece, they also brought many benefits. They built roads, undertook irrigation schemes, even encouraged tourism, so that at least no islanders starved under their occupation, as many would have done, had the islands been left entirely to their own resources. In particular, the Italians' great service to Rhodes was their partial afforestation of the island. It must be hard for anyone strolling through the lovely woods of Profitis Elias on Rhodes to realize that these cypresses, plane trees, pine and fir trees were once the norm on every Greek island. The practice of shipbuilding has taken a terrible toll.

Common products of all the Dodecanese today are grapes, citrus fruits, peaches, figs and, of course, the ubiquitous olive. Wherever the olive grows in southern Europe, people always seem able to make a living.

Some of the hardest—and also the happiest—days for these islands have been in living memory. In 1943 German troops took over the then Italian islands, only to be dislodged by the British in 1945 after some bitter fighting. In 1947 a UNO decree reunited the islands with the Greek motherland, after centuries of separation.

As far as the tourist is concerned, the only reminder of the long separation will be in the tax and customs regulations obtaining on these islands, which mean that a whole series of foreign goods—ranging from fur coats to whisky—are sold at relatively low prices. Best of all, the vehicle-owner can fill his tank more cheaply here than anywhere else in Greece.

Rhodes—World Meeting-Place and Island of Sun

So great is the wealth of historical interest, the variety of sports and entertainments, and the richness of natural beauty of this island, that it needs a book of its own to do it justice. Fortunately, there is just such a book in this series (**Rhodes**, by Franck Weimert), and those meaning to spend any length of

time on the island are strongly advised to get it. But for those
whose visit may be only short, the following is a brief guide
to the main attractions.

As with most Greek islands, the ancient history of Rhodes is
a blend of fact and fiction, of legend and actuality. According
to legend, the island was a gift from Zeus to Apollo the Sun-
god, who named it Rhodos after the nymph he was currently
courting. It is also often called The Island of Roses, referring
to the oleander or laurel rose which grows profusely here.

First colonized by Minoans and Mycenaeans, Rhodes only
became prosperous after the settlement of Dorian Greeks in
the island in the 11th century B.C. They founded three cities—
Ialissos, Kamiros and Lindos. The island became an important
commercial crossroads between East and West, and in the 5th
century B.C. the three cities got together to found an administrative center near the site of the modern capital. This became
a flourishing nucleus of culture and the arts.

Competition with Rome led to the end of Rhodes's prosperity,
and it remained unimportant until the 14th century. It was
then, however, that a great new chapter opened in the life of
this balmy isle. For in 1306, the Genoese, who then held
Rhodes, sold it to the crusading Knights of St. John, who had
been driven from the Holy Land by the Muslims. These
doughty warriors fortified the entire island, and for 200 years
held the Muslim armies at bay. But in 1522, the Knights were
forced out, and the story of the island becomes that of the
whole of the Dodecanese.

The popularity of the island as a tourist center springs from
many sources—only one of which is its unique blend of a
romantic and very visible past with all modern facilities. Another unique feature is its climate—the most temperate in
Greece, with a winter average temperature around 62°F. (16—
17°C.) and cooling breezes in summer. Its vegetation is pro-
fuse and varied—oleander, broom, myrtle, lavender and sage
mingle with woods of pine, oak and cypress. There is a variety
of small mammals—deer, foxes, hedgehogs and badgers among
others, while the island is famed for its profusion of butterflies,
especially in spring.

The island is extremely easy to reach. There are direct flights
from London, England, twice a week, by BEA and Olympic
Airways. From Athens, there are daily flights all year, with
5 departures a day in the high season. If you wish to bring
your own automobile, there are car ferry facilities on a regular
basis from Genoa and Naples in Italy, and from Marseilles in

southern France. By sea, there are regular services from Piraeus—or you could start from Marseilles, Venice or Trieste.

Once you have reached the island, here are some of the chief attractions for a quick visit.

Rhodes, the capital, really consists of two towns, the medieval and the modern. The Old Town is entirely enclosed within the immensely powerful walls of the Knights' stronghold. You can walk along the top of the walls, and get a good view of the town layout. The streets are full of colorful reminders of the multi-national crusaders. In the Turkish quarter are minarets and barred windows dating from the days of Turkish occupation. Encircling the Old Town is the new, modern Rhodes, with a wide choice of good hotels, night clubs, a casino (at the Grand Hotel), heated swimming pools, and shops selling goods at duty-free prices. Rhodian specialities on sale are brightly colored ceramics and silver Rhodian jewellery. The harbor of the New Town is called Mandraki. It was this harbor entrance which once was straddled by the famed Colossus of Rhodes, a bronze statue of Apollo, some 126 feet high, and weighing, it is calculated 300 tons.

Other spots of major interest on Rhodes are as follows:

— Just over a mile from the capital, topping a hill known as Mount Smith, are the ruins of the ancient acropolis, dating from the 2nd century B.C.

— About 5 miles south of Rhodes city is Kalithie, with a fine beach nearby. This is a spa resort, with therapeutic waters, and a blend of Turkish and Greek architecture.

— Ialissos—the first of the three ancient cities mentioned— is about 5-1/2 miles south-west of the capital. Though little now remains to show of the B.C. city, there is a beautiful 15th century monastery on the acropolis hill; the crypt contains 14th-15th century frescoes.

— Kamiros, the second ancient city, lies 15-1/2 miles beyond Ialissos, on the west coast. There are extensive ruins on wooded slopes overlooking the sea. To be seen are houses, streets, a 3rd century B.C. temple and colonnade, a 5th century cistern.

— Lindos, described by most travel writers as a "must" has, unlike the other two ancient cities, been continuously occupied since the days of its foundation. It lies south-south-west of and about 21 miles from the capital, at the

end of a delightful drive along the east coast. In Dorian
days it had been the main port of the island and a center
of the cult of the goddess Athene, to whom temples
were constantly built and rebuilt on the Acropolis. In the
15th century the Knights of St. John built a powerful fort
on a crag here. The Apostle Paul landed close by. The
4th century Temple of Athene at Lindos is one of the most
beautiful in Greece.

— The Valley of the Butterflies is about 16 miles south of
Rhodes city. There is a thickly wooded gorge where, each
spring, thousands of butterflies settle on the trees, attracted
by.aromatic gums.

From the capital there are regular bus services to most parts
of the island. Numerous self-drive automobile hire firms
have offices in Rhodes city, including Hertz and Avis. A
number of agencies rent sail-boats and motor-boats. During
the season there are multi-lingual "Sound and Light" entertainments in the capital, and Greek folk theater and dancing
displays. At Rodini there is a wine festival from July 15th
to September 30th. The car rally of Rhodes, involving a
circuit of the island, starts on July 28th. These are only
some of the highlights of the pleasures and entertainments
offered by this island. If you are contemplating visiting
the island on a specific date, enquire from your national
Greek Tourist Organization Office (see ADDRESSES pages)
for brochures giving details of festivals and events. There
is also a main office of the National Tourist Organization
of Greece (E.O.T.) at Archiepiskopou Makariou and Papagou
Corner in Rhodes city.

Kos—Birthplace of Hippocrates

After Rhodes, this is the best-known of the Dodecanese
Islands. Covering about 112 square miles, it stretches some
31 miles along its main axis, but is never more than 5-6
miles in breadth. About half the population of 18,000 live
in the capital, Kos.

As it constitutes one of the halts for shipping sailing from
Piraeus to Rhodes, Kos can be reached daily from the Greek
capital. There is also a frequent air service from Athens
(5 times weekly) by Olympic Airways: Kos airport is about
12 miles south of the capital, near the village of Antimahia.
There are also frequent boat excursions to the island from
neighboring isles, especially Rhodes. The nearest Turkish
port with regular boat services is Bodrun—but be warned
that fares involving crossing the frontier between Greece

and Turkey will seem disproportionately high. The shipping agents in Kos all have offices close to the capital's harbor.

If you arrive by sea, the first thing that will strike you will be the castle of the Knights of St. John to the left of Kos town harbor. Much has been done in recent years to rescue this mid-15th century citadel from eventual decay. Completion of its construction was achieved by Grand Master del Caretto in 1514—i.e., just a few years before it fell into the hands of the Turks, anyway! At many points, coats of arms have been chiselled into the walls, to remind the medieval populace of the sovereignty of the knights of Rhodes. Kos is particularly fertile, and Rhodes obtained a large proportion of its provender from the island. Right from antiquity, Kos has been regarded as a sort of supermarket-garden of the Aegean.

A narrow arm of the sea separates the castle from the city. On the landward side is Platanou Square, in which grows the celebrated Plane Tree of Hippocrates, a giant tree under which the great physician of antiquity was supposed to have taught. Whether you believe it or not, it is delightful to sit there, close to a charming Turkish fountain.

Like Rhodes, Kos contains many mementoes of its former Turkish (and Italian) masters. One example, in the same square, is the Loggia Mosque. Behind the mosque lies the ancient harbor quarter of Kos, most of it excavated after 1933.

Also worth looking at, in the same area, are parts of the town fortifications, on the eastern side; nearby, the remains of a small temple—possibly to Hercules—and, to the west, a larger Temple of Aphrodite. Farther west still is the covered colonnade of the ancient market (*aghora*), some 160 yards in length by 86 yards wide. In the same area you will find mosaics which have been covered over to protect them from sand and shingle. But you may move the covering aside, to expose the gentle colors and harmonies of the designs.

If you leave the excavations above the harbor by way of the *aghora*, you will come to the Platia Eleftherias, with the 18th century Defterdar Mosque. Nearby is the museum, open from 9 a.m. to 1 p.m., then from 2 p.m. to 5 p.m. It contains some interesting exhibits, such as a reconstruction of a Roman inner courtyard, with a mosaic showing the arrival of Aesculapius on Kos. There is also a statue

of Hippocrates, who was born on Kos, and one of Artemis
of Ephesus, dating from around the 2nd century B.C. This
is the "Diana of the Ephesians" mentioned in the mission-
ary journeys of Saint Paul, a multi-breasted goddess of
fertility (Diana was the name given by the Romans to the
Greek goddess Artemis).

Carry on along the Vass-Paulou Avenue, and you will
reach the Roman baths and Casa Romana. These buildings
both testify to the fact that this must have been quite a
popular resort of the Romans, though the earthquakes in
the 6th century are believed to have brought the *dolce
vita* to an end. The hypocaust is particularly well preserved in the baths, while there are some beautiful mosaics
in the villa (especially the Sea Picture with Fish). Many
fine mosaics have been removed to the Grand Master's
Palace on Rhodes.

From the Casa Romana it is only a short distance to the
ancient Theater, in which classical dramas are still sometimes presented. The upper seven rows of seats are believed
to date from the Hellenistic period.

On the opposite side of the road is the second major excavation site of Kos town. The best place to start a visit
to the site is by the old acropolis, distinguishable today
by a tall minaret erected there. Much here will remind the
Italian traveler of Pompeii. Of particular interest is a 100-
yard stretch of Roman paved road, flanked by the remains
of Roman houses. Note especially the House of Europa,
which still contains a fine mosaic showing Europa and the
Bull, although most of the mosaic-work has been removed
to the museum. Behind this building stands a large Roman
baths, which contain some Greek columns and also traces
of an early Christian basilica.

But the best-known antiquity of this island is undoubtedly
the Asklepieion, a shrine to Aesculapius, the Greek god of
the art of medicine. It is one of the most beautifully situ-
ated ancient shrines in the Aegean. It is best reached by
taxi from Kos, being about 3 miles from the city outskirts.
Unless you're particularly tired, you can dismiss the taxi,
as the way back is all downhill.

Aesculapius was regarded as a god with quite exceptional
powers—even able to bring back people from the under-
world of Hades. He is generally represented by serpents,
which the Greeks believed had the ability to discover healing
herbs, and was most venerated on Kos and at Epidaurus, on
the Greek mainland. His followers, a closed order of priests

called Asklepiadai, practiced medicine along the lines laid down by Hippocrates. As is well known, the Hippocratic Oath, which was binding on the pupils of the physician, is still regarded as one of the foundation stones of medical ethics.

It appears that building of the Asklepieion began after the death of Hippocrates in the 4th century B.C. Distributed over four levels, the shrine was one of the great places of veneration of ancient Greece. At the lowest level are the remains of some Roman baths. On the next level up were the hospitalization precincts. With its magnificent setting among cypress and pine groves and its grand view over the sea, it is easy to see this as an area allotted for healing. There are the remains of three rows of colonnades, which possibly constituted a kind of foyer for the former patients. There is a delightful fountain here, running with fresh spring water, and, nearby, the remains of a temple to Xenophon.

The main flight of steps to the next level leads directly to the remains of an Aesculapian altar, and close by, seven marble columns of a Temple to Apollo in the Ionic style, partly reconstructed by the Italians. To the right of the altar is the Ionic Temple of Aesculapius, much simpler in construction than the Apollo Temple.

The next flight of steps are among the most majestic remaining from antiquity. They are divided into three stages. On the middle stage was formerly an altar: this leads to the uppermost stage of all—on which the mighty Doric temple of Aesculapius was built in the 2nd century B.C. It is the crowning glory of the Asklepieion, but would nevertheless have remained unknown to us, had it not been for dedicated work by the German archaeologist Herzog, at the beginning of this century. He uncovered the remains, and the Italians completed the revelation you now see, by careful reconstructions.

If you intend to stay longer on Kos, you will certainly want to make longer trips from the capital. There are some particularly beautiful landscapes on the island. In this respect, the local bus services will only be of use if you are ready to travel with a grip containing overnight gear. At the same time, there are also organized trips, which will bring you back to your own hotel bed each evening. It is also possible to hire automobiles and scooters—though, judging from what I have seen, I would not recommend hiring the latter for use outside built-up areas.

Here are some brief notes on some of the best excursions:

— About 6 miles behind the capital, turn left in the village of Gipari, into delightful mountainous country. By way of Asfendiou, you reach Mount Diakros (3,000 feet), the island's highest peak. On the way back, take a right turn in Gipari, for a good beach at Tingakion.

— About 7-1/2 miles out from the capital, take a left turn for Pilion. In the village, ask for directions to Amaniou, about 1-1/4 miles away over field tracks. From here, you can reach the ruins of Old Pilion, with a Byzantine castle and a ruined church containing 15th century frescoes.

— Close to present-day Pilion is the so-called Charmyleion, of uncertain origin. As you leave Pilion, it is behind a little settlement to the left, called Charmeli. In the burial chamber of a Byzantine Chapel are twelve stone coffins—which, according to local legend, contain the bones of the 12 apostles.

— From Pilion, take the road to Kardamena, a pretty little fishing village which is a favorite Greek holiday resort. There is a good beach just outside the township. There are excellent restaurants here, and good hotels or private accommodation, if you need to stay overnight. You will generally find a vacancy without difficulty, except in the peak months of June-August.

— If you stay overnight, go back the following day by way of Antimahia, with its splendid forts. An unusual feature here is a fortress built on a triangular plan by Grand Master of the Knights of St. John, Pierre d'Aubusson (1476-1505). The interior is poorly preserved, but the view from the battlements makes the ascent worthwhile.

— Some 11 miles west of here lies the near-coastal village of Kefalos. If you notice a turning to the left, this will take you via a very uneven road to the magnificent Bay of Kefalos. At Astypalaia, near Kefalos, Hippocrates, the greatest son of the island, was born in the 5th century B.C.

Kalimnos—Home of the Sponge Fishers

The northern neighbor of Kos is the much smaller Kalimnos—reached by ships from Piraeus en route for Rhodes, or by boat from a nearby Dodecanese island. Kalimnos covers about 23 square miles, but has a population of some 14,000. Of this number, about 10,000 live in the capital, also called Kalimnos, or, alternatively, Pothia.

Before you reach the wide harbor you will see straight
away there is no lush vegetation here, as on Rhodes and
Kos. Left and right, barren rocks plunge into the sea. It
may seem a bleak prospect, but for the walker with a taste
for the unusual, this island has many exciting possibilities.
On Kalimnos you enter a strange, hilly, almost tree-less
world, which you can enjoy best if you choose a date
remote from the hot summer months. Best of all is the
end of April/early May or from mid-September on.

But though, at first sight, the island seems largely barren,
there are two quite fertile valleys. Moreover, the capital
has an air of prosperity about it. But this prosperity is
based, not on the island's wealth of produce, but on its
well-known sponge-fishing activities, based on the harbor
of Pothia, as the capital is most frequently called. It is
from here that the island's celebrated sponge-fisher fleet
has sailed since time immemorial.

The use of sponge was as well-known in antiquity as the
use of plastic sponge or rubber sponge is today. Homer
mentions its many uses—in Odysseus's castle it was employed
to wash down the dining tables, and the blacksmith-god
Vulcan wiped his hands with sponge. It is also suggested
that some of the heavy armor worn by the Greek heroes
was padded with the substance.

From antiquity until quite recently, sponges were collected
in shallow waters in the same risky and demanding fashion.
The diver fixed a heavy stone to his chest, which quickly
took him to the sea bed. He uprooted the sponges with a
trident, and on giving a signal was drawn to the surface by
ropes. But the modern sponge diver uses a rubber suit
and prefers the deeper waters off the North African shores.

Nevertheless, it is still from Pothia harbor that the sponge
fleet leaves. Early in April there is a festival before it sets
off, and a much livelier one in September to celebrate its
safe return. You can buy fine sponges in the streets of the
capital—but don't expect any exceptionally low price.

The little capital has a charming quayside, with a bell
tower, near to the Aghios Christos Church. A particularly good buy is Kalimnos honey, over which Ovid rhapsodized in his love poems: it is still good today.

If you intend to stay more than a day, here are some
enjoyable trips:

— To the Vottuni Caves, reached by boat from the capital, followed by a climb on mules. These are stalactite and stalagmite caves, in ancient days a shrine to Zeus. Another good cave lies between the capital and Vathis, the Daskaleios Cave. To get there, bribe a boatman from Vathis on a fine day to take you there: it is not easy of access.

— To Vathis, reached from the capital over land or by boat. It is surrounded by orange groves, which shed a delicious fragrance in spring.

— To Horion (or Chorion), north of the capital, below the 2,300 feet high Mount Profitis Elias. In the neighborhood, a crusaders' castle.

— To Linaria, in the north-west of the island, with fine, sandy beaches.

— To Myrthies, a hamlet some 5 miles from Pothia, and a little farther on, to Masouri, with simple accommodation facilities and pleasant *tavernas*, also a fine, sandy beach.

— From Myrthies, take a boat to the nearby islet of Telendos, a 1,300 feet high rocky clump. The crossing takes about 15 minutes. In the narrow straits between the islands an American research team found the remains of a sunken city, presumably the victim of an earthquake.

Simi—Home of the Fairest King

Simi (often spelt Syme in English texts), lies just north of the island of Rhodes, in a gulf of the Turkish mainland. According to Homer, it supplied the fairest of the Greek kings to go to the Trojan War. But apparently the fair king was also a dreadful coward, and had little following.

Covering about 20 square miles, the island has a population of about 3,000, most of them living in the same-name capital, Simi. The town stretches up a hill from the harbor to the remains of the acropolis and a Crusaders' castle. In antiquity the town was called Aigianos: today, the harbor area is popularly known as Gialos.

The island can be reached by a daily shipping connection from Piraeus. Further, during the season, there are almost daily trips to Simi from Rhodes or Kos. The fame of the island in antiquity rested on the Simians' skill in boat-building. They were especially known for their production of light skiffs, a craft that also commended itself to the Knights of St. John, who liked to use these light vessels for raiding trips in the eastern Aegean. The island is also known for its sponge divers.

If you wish to stay a little longer here, you can either find accommodation in the capital, or put up at the Aghios Michaele Monastery in Panormltls, on the southernmost tip of the island. Pleasant excursions can be made to the little health resort of Emborio, to the west of the capital, and the little Monastery of Roukomotti.

Particular feast days on this island are Easter, and November 7th-9th each year.

Astipalea—Almost One of the Cyclades

The farthest west of the Dodecanese, this butterfly-shaped island seems geographically more one of the Cyclades. A glance at the map will show its position and extraordinary shape—two "wings" joined by a four-mile long "body" that, in places, is little more than 100 yards wide. The overall area of the island is just under 40 square miles; its population, about 1,500. Locals also call their island Astropalia or Stampalia, but the spelling given in the title here is that used by the Greek National Tourist Organization.

Most of the inhabitants of Astipalea live in the same-name capital at the south-west end. As with Kea, the island is said to have 200 churches—but here it seems to be true. Most of them are small, attractive, and decorated with icons. A mighty castle, built by the Venetian Quirini family early in the 13th century dominates the capital.

In Roman times, the protected bays of Astipalea were popular retreats for their ships. Today, this is less the case—in fact the island can only be reached by occasional ships from Piraeus traveling to the Dodecanese. The maximum frequency one may expect is once a week from Piraeus, but there are generally plenty of opportunities of access by way of a *caïque* from one of the neighboring isles of the group.

But if the island is difficult to reach, it offers some marvellous advantages to the keen bather—crystal-clear water, and fine, sandy beaches on either side of the narrow isthmus, close to the capital. There are a few island taxis, but mainly it is an island which offers delightful opportunities for people who enjoy peaceful rambles, have some basic knowledge of modern Greek, and can do without heated swimming pools and other sophistications. There are a number of simple hotels and private rooming-houses. The best excursion is to Maltezana Bay, in the south-east .

Leros—The Woman's Island

This title has nothing to do with the balance of population or Women's Lib. It is simply that, on this island, since the mists of antiquity, priority of inheritance is the privilege of women. Generally speaking, houses and property go to the eldest daughter, on the death of the owner. This rule, exceptional in modern times, seems to date right back to early days of civilization, when matriarchy rather than patriarchy was the rule—the world was more commonly thought to be controlled by a Mother-God than by a Father-God figure. Only the remoteness of the island has enabled it to keep this tradition unsullied by more male-oriented cultures.

Lying north-west of Kalimnos, the island covers some 19 square miles, and is about 8-3/4 miles long with a maximum width of 4-1/2 miles. The heavily-indented coastline provides numerous bays. Of the island's 6,500 inhabitants, somewhat under a half (c. 2,700) live in the capital, Platanos, with its harbor Aghia Marina. The passenger boats, however, dock in Lakion (also known as Porto Lakki), in the west of the island. This harbor lies at the end of a deep bay, and, for that reason, was to have been developed as a naval base—especially by the Italians, who seem to have over-rated its potentialities.

If you arrive at Lakion, your best plan is to take a taxi directly to the capital, which is about 2-1/2 miles to the east. The main attraction here is a fort, expanded by the Knights of St. John from a Byzantine foundation. It can be reached by road, or up seemingly endless flights of steps. From here you get a splendid view of the island.

The best way to explore Leros in detail is with the aid of a friendly taxi-driver. But don't expect the impossible! On such an island it will be a miracle if you meet anyone speaking good English. You must have a few Greek phrases, at least, at your command, to make your wishes known.

All the best trips on Leros are to bays. In the south there is Xirokampos; in the west, Gourna; in the north, to the left of the little settlement of Aghia Matrona, there is the Virgin's Bay, Ormos Parthai. At the western end of this bay are the ruins of a Temple of Artemis, the perpetually chaste goddess, who was worshipped here in the form of a guinea-fowl.

Patmos—Scene of the Revelation of St. John

Until my curiosity was fired by a fellow-traveler on Rhodes, I had always thought of Patmos simply as the island to which the Roman Emperors sent citizens condemned to banishment. But a chance meeting with a German woman visitor who had come regularly to Patmos for ten years and rhapsodized over the island, sent me hurrying to the steamer the following morning.

Patmos is served by shipping lines from Piraeus en route for Rhodes. To get to Patmos from the larger island, you simply catch a boat making the return journey. After stops at Kos and Kalimnos, the steamer ties up in Skala, the fjord-like harbor inlet of Patmos, late in the evening. As usual in the islands, incoming steamers are greeted by groups of local folk offering accommodation. I soon found a room and spent the rest of that evening in a nearby *taverna*.

Once again, I found that cordiality of welcome which makes such a contrast between the smaller islands and the larger tourist centers. And I repeat my earlier advice: when traveling in the Aegean, don't be too concerned to seek for luxury and endless so-called "facilities". The beauty of the landscape, and the genuine warmth of welcome you're more likely to get in the less frequented areas more than outweigh such sophisticated advantages.

Patmos is the northernmost of the islands belonging to the *Nomos* or Administrative District of the Dodecanese. In earlier centuries it tended to be grouped with the Cyclades, while during the years of suzerainty of the Knights of St. John on Rhodes, Patmos and Leros had formed a joint monastic state under the protection of the Venetian Dukedom of Naxòs. The island covers some 13 square miles, and has a population of around 2,500.

The main townships are the harbor town of Skala (population 1,000) and the 1-1/4 miles distant capital, Patmos, with a similar number of inhabitants. The capital lies about 850 feet above sea level, and here is the main point of interest for the visitor, the Monastery of Saint John. According to tradition, the beloved disciple wrote not only his gospel while on the island, but also the book known to Protestants as "The Book of Revelation" and to Roman Catholics as "The Apocalypse", those visions of the future of Christendom which defy all precise interpretation.

As a matter of historical fact, the Emperor Domitian did exile to this island a Christian named John in the year 95, after an incident at nearby Ephesus in Asia Minor. It is said that, once here, the apostle dictated his writings to a disciple, Prochoros. The grotto where this is supposed to have taken place lies between Skala and the capital, and can be visited. The apostle's own reference is found in the first chapter of the book of his revelations: "I, John, your brother, and a sharer with you in the sorrows and Kingship and patient endurance of Jesus, found myself in the island of Patmos, on account of the Word of God and the truth told us by Jesus. . . . "

The grotto, now known as The Grotto of the Apocalypse, lies a little higher than the Theological Seminary, which you will pass on your way to the capital. It forms part of some large church precincts which contain, among other objects, a beautiful icon of the patron saint. In the grotto are the rock said to have served as his writing-desk, and a stone, now embedded in silver, said to have been the saint's pillow.

The great Monastery of Saint John towers high over the capital. For all its theological intentions, however, this was also a very strong fortress which long frustrated enemy efforts to capture this key point in the Aegean. The monastery was founded in 1088 by Blessed Christodoulos, a noted scholar of the day, by permission of the Byzantine Emperor Alexis. Preserved in the monastery's archives you can see the document granting Christodoulos tenure of the island, possession of a ship for the community, and the monastery's perpetual freedom from taxation. Patmos was late to come under Turkish domination, until it was occupied by the Italians in 1912.

Most of the monastic building dates from the 15th century. It was erected on the site of a former large Byzantine basilica, which, in its turn, had used the stones of a previous Temple of Artemis built on the spot. Apart from Sundays and Church Feast Days, when it is open only from 8-12 in the morning, you may visit the monastery on any weekday. You enter the building between two mighty towers. Over the portal is a little balcony, from which boiling oil or water could be poured on troublesome besiegers. From the gate you reach first a central inner court, then the outer forecourt (Narthex), where there are frescoes showing the Evangelist on Patmos.

To the right is a chapel dedicated to the monastery's founders, containing the remains of Blessed Christodoulos;

to the left is an inner court with an 11th century icon of
Saint John. To the right of the main church is a four-
column domed church, with a fine floor and early 19th
century iconostasis. Through a door to the right in the
Chapel of Mary you reach an inner court leading to the
refectory. This is an impressive hall, with two marble
tables beneath a dome. To the south and slightly lower
is the church.

North of the refectory is the monastery's Treasure
Chamber. The greatest treasures here are the ancient
books and manuscripts. Soon after its foundation, Blessed
Christodoulos began to gather to the monastery library
a rich collection of ancient books and manuscripts, and
these now constitute the greatest valuables of the island.
Christodoulos set his monks to make inventories of the
manuscripts and to copy them. Their number was constantly increased by gifts and today the collection
numbers some 1,000 manuscripts, numerous incunabula,
and about 10,000 documents.

Of particular beauty in the Treasure Chamber is a 6th
century Gospel of Saint Mark. It is written in silver letter-
ing resembling filigree work, with the names of Jesus Christ
and the Saints in gold. Look particularly at the marvellous
work on page 80 (11th century) and page 81 (19th century), showing scenes from the life of Saint John.

From the monastery's roof terrace you have a magnificent
view of the whole island. From here you can see quite
clearly how it is composed of three laval masses, separated
from one another by deep bays.

If you decide on a longer stay on Patmos, you may be sure
of a happy time. Not only is there ample accommodation
in the north of the island, but in recent years several hotels
of the better class have been opened. Feast Days to note
are: May 21st—Feast of Saint John; on March 16th and
October 21st, feasts are held in honor of Blessed Christodoulos.

Among favorite excursions are the following:

— To Grikon, with numerous hotels and a fine beach.

— To the Isthmus of Stavrös. Around here are a great many
enticing beaches. One small snag—there are a great many
sea urchins around, and you are advised to wear swimming
shoes in the water.

— To Kambos Bay, on the north-east coast of the island, reached in 2 hours on foot, possibly more quickly by boat—depending on the weather.

— One of the most enjoyable excursions is a boat tour of the entire island. There are always opportunities for this, starting from Skala. Be sure to take food with you, and persuade your boatman to make a stop at one of the lovely bays in the west of the island—Minika or Kipos ton Ossion.

Karpathos—A 'Plane Flight Back into the Middle Ages

This title should not cause any misgivings. You do not emerge from your aircraft, at the airport close to the capital, into a grey world of the past. But for anyone interested, a stay on Karpathos gives the opportunity of studying at first hand scenes of communal life which have changed little since the earliest societies. The folk costumes worn everywhere by the islanders are not just assumed for the benefit of tourists!

Along with its sister isles of Saria (uninhabited), to the north, and Kassos, to the south-west, the 116 square miles of Karpathos form part of a chain linking Rhodes and Crete with the European and Asia Minor mainlands.

Karpathos is about 30 miles long, and up to 5-1/2 miles in width; it is 40 miles from Crete to the east and 30 miles from Rhodes to the north-west. Immediately on arrival, you will see by the numerous Italian-style buildings that this island is one of the Dodecanese, and belonged to the early 20th century Italian *Impero*. Nevertheless, its situation between two larger islands which have always been much more attractive to expansionist powers, has guaranteed Karpathos a relatively peaceful history.

The island's greatest period was in antiquity, when it was known successively as Tripolis, Tetrapolis, Hetapolis, and finally Oktopolis (meaning 3-, 4-, 7- and 8-towns respectively), as it grew in importance. In medieval times it was first subject to Genoa, then to Venice, until, in 1538, it was overrun by the dreaded Turkish pirate, Barbarossa. Karpathos then remained under Turkish domination until 1912, when it joined the reunited Greece.

The capital town is Karpathos, also known as Pighadia, in the south-east. Nearby is the site of the ancient capital, Poseidonion.

The island's highest peak is Mount Kalolimno, rising to almost 4,000 feet. Those who have climbed it tell me the
sight from the top is unforgettable, especially in early morning, when the light effects are enchanting. The Italians did
a good job here—as on Rhodes— by their afforestation
program.

From the capital, the following trips can be made:

— By bus to Aperion, home of the episcopal church of the
island. From here, there is a path with fantastic views up
to the village of Volada.

— Another route from the capital takes you via Menete to
Arkassa. One of the most remarkable spots on the island,
Arkassa was the capital during the time of Venetian domination. There is an early Byzantine basilica and signs of
Venetian-style buildings. The beautiful silver ornaments
often worn by the women here, and sometimes offered for
sale, probably date from a tradition of Venetian times. On
the island there are both iron mines and silver mines—the
latter celebrated since antiquity.

Any fertility of which the island can boast is confined to
its southern half. Around the capital, the Bay of Vronti,
and Lastos are areas known for their production of fruit
and vegetables. Right in the south are orange trees and
fine wild quince. Do not fail to try the quince jelly sold
here.

The mountainous north of the island is scarcely developed
for tourism. But those who don't mind walking and are in-
trigued by primitive customs, should seriously consider a
trip to the village of Olibos (or Olimbos) in the north. It is
said to be the oldest community on the island, where many
ancient customs are preserved, and even traces of the ancient
Doric Greek language have remained in the people's dialect.

The folk costumes worn by the women here are not, as on
more tourist-oriented islands, put on to impress visitors,
but are the normal day-to-day wear of the inhabitants. The
women wear a bright blouse, embroidered over the breast,
and over it a long dark blue coat, also richly decorated with
needlework. A three-cornered head scarf, colored stockings
and shoes complete the picture.

High points of the villagers' life are the weddings. These
generally last about three days, and are preceded by weeks
of preparation. The feast begins with enchanting songs,
dedicated to the bride; then, to the accompaniment of
more music, the groom appears and leads his bride to the

church. Some 800 guests may gather for the occasion, eating at long tables in the open air. A feature of the feast is that the women may only take food when the men have already eaten their fill.

But if you are privileged to witness such a spectacle, you should dismiss all previous 'folksy' ideas from your mind. These people are not playing games for the benefit of tourists—or even for their own benefit. Their customs stem from very old and meaningful traditions in a society whose members are committed to a pretty stark existence from their earliest years. A little girl is introduced to weaving at the age of ten, and by the time she may think of marriage will have laboriously woven her entire dowry. Obviously, you will get no profound view of tradition here, in the course of a flying visit. If your interest is serious, you will need to stay several weeks in the community— where you will find that classic hospitality for which ancient Greece was famed. Then it is up to you—by your conduct—to win confidence and friends, and so a deeper insight into the outlook and customs of the people.

The best way to get to Olibos from the capital is by motor launch to the small harbor of Diafanion: the trip will take about two hours. After landing, the distance to the village is about 6 miles over a somewhat rough road. Alternatively, you may travel to Olibos overland from Volada. The overall distance by this route is about 19 miles from the capital, and you are advised to hire a mule or donkey.

Warning. On Greek Tourist Organization maps, the name of the village appears as Olibos, as given here. But you may find it variously named Olimbos or Olimpos or even Olympos!

Just off the northern tip of Karpathos, separated by a channel only 100 feet wide, through which courses an extremely strong current, lies the uninhabited isle of Saria. Off the southern tip is Kassos island, some 25 square miles in area, with a population of 1,400. The capital of the latter is Fri, founded in 1840. To the south and east the coastline is steep. But to the south-east of the lighthouse (just north-east of Aghia Marina) there are fine, sandy beaches, as on the tiny uninhabited islet of Armathia opposite.

If Karpathos's history had been relatively uneventful, its sister isle Kassos suffered considerably in the Greek Wars of Independence early in the 19th century. Following an uprising in 1824, most of the island's male population were massacred by the Turks, and over 2,000 women and children were carried off as slaves. Later, many Kassiots were to be found engaged in the construction of the Suez Canal, and many of their descendants became pilots through its waters.

Chapter Nine

CRETE—"THE FAIR AND FERTILE"

Crete, "the fair and fertile, circled by the sea", as Homer described it, is, like Rhodes, so rich in historic, artistic and scenic interest that it needs a book of its own to describe it fully. In the following paragraphs, an attempt has been made to give at least an outline portrait of this unique island.

Crete, known into the 18th century as Chania, and today by the Greeks themselves as Kriti, is unique from the point of view of size, position, history and people. As to the last, St. Paul quotes somewhat unkindly, in his letter to Titus, the words of one of their own prophets, that "Cretans are always liars, dangerous animals, idle gluttons". "This testimony" continues Paul "is true." But whatever St. Paul may have thought, it was certainly not the opinion of antiquity, where Crete was regarded as a happy isle, an island of the blessed, chosen by Zeus as the venue for his marriage to Hera, to which he later abducted the Princess Europa, and where she produced a number of children for him.

Crete—Its Form

Largest of the Greek Islands, fourth largest in the Mediterranean, Crete has an area around 3,200 square miles, a coastline over 600 miles long, and a maximum length of 160 miles: the width varies from 7-1/2 to 37 miles.

Geologically, the island is part of a limestone chain linking the Greek Peloponnese with Rhodes and the Asia Minor mainland. In the west are the White Mountains (Lefka Ori), rising to a maximum 8,700 feet; centrally, there is Mount Idi (8,000 feet); to the east are the Dikti Mountains (up to 7,000 feet).

The north coast comprises numerous large bays, which are backed by fertile plains and valleys. The largest agricultural area is the 60 square miles of the Mesara Plain, south-west of Mount Idi. Mainland products of the island are wine, raisins, tomatoes, vegetables, melons, wheat and barley.

Another unique feature of Crete is its position—mid-way between mainland Europe, mainland Asia Minor, and the North African coast.

Crete—Its History

The origins of the people of Crete may well have stemmed from some 3,000 years B.C., when wandering tribes from Asia Minor met North African tribes on this island, and mingled with them to form a fresh race. These early Cretans evidently worked in copper and were skilled ship-builders. Burial places and clay pottery from this period are said to be from the Early Minoan or pre-Palace Period, dated between 2,600 and 2,000 B.C. This is followed by the Middle Minoan or Early Palace Period (from c. 2,000–1700 B.C.), and lastly by the Late Minoan or Later Palace Period (1,700-1,400 B.C.).

The most significant evidences of Minoan culture all date from this 600 years between 2,000 and 1,400 B.C. During this period the Palace of Knossos was built near present-day Herakleion, also the Palace of Phaistos, about 40 miles to the south-west, the Palace of Malia, 22 miles east of Herakleion, and the Palace of Kalo Zakros, first excavated in 1962, in the middle of the far-distant east coast.

The most significant finds have been these:

— vases of all shapes and sizes, and for all purposes;

— statuettes;
— jewellery and ornaments of all kinds; and
— frescoes giving a most lively impression of the ideals and life-style of the people.

The best display of Minoan art is in Herakleion Archaeological Museum.

Throughout this 600 years, palaces were constantly destroyed and rebuilt or partly rebuilt following earthquakes. This went on until, at a certain point in the 15th century B.C., the whole fabric of Minoan civilization abruptly disappears.

Until recent years, no light could be cast on this abrupt end to what must have been a flourishing civilization. But those who have read the chapter on Santorin Island (q.v.) in the Cyclades will have an idea of the explanation which has now largely replaced older theories of conquest by superior forces. Spiro Marinatos was among the first to theorize that the great volcanic explosion which took place at Santorin, (70 miles north), in the 15th century B.C., also gave rise to a tidal wave and subsequent earthquakes which completely wiped out the civilization of the Crete of those days. For this had been a thalassocracy, a maritime empire, dependent for its survival on a strong fleet— and this would have been entirely eliminated by such a disaster.

After this all-time catastrophe only the Palace of Knossos was rebuilt—but the evidence is that this rebuilding was carried out by an entirely fresh power, in fact by Mycenaeans emigrating from the Greek mainland. The clue to this was given in a hoard of ancient clay tablets discovered by English archaeologist Sir Arthur Evans (1851-1941).

Evans divided the writing tablets into three periods:

— Minoan hieroglyphics (2,000-1,750 B.C.);
— Linear Script A (1,750-1,450 B.C.); and
— Linear Script B (a development of Script A, and, in Crete, found only at Knossos).

Over 4,000 tablets were found, so hardened by a fire that the symbols remain readable to this day. Readable, but for long undecipherable. Then, in 1939, at the Palace of Nestor in the Peloponnese a find was made of 608 tablets in the Cretan script of Linear B—comprising a document from the time of the Trojan War.

Clarification of these finds is owed to a young Anglo-Greek, Michael Ventris, who, using decodification methods

developed in the World War, broke the cipher of Linear **B**
He found that Linear B actually enshrined in writing the
speech of the early Greeks. What had happened was that
Mycenaeans, tracking to Crete after the Great Catastrophe
had used the symbols used by the Minoans (i.e. the
symbols of Linear B), to set down their own early Greek
tongue in writing. Linear B had 88 characters, and this
was easier to master than, for example, Egyptian, with
over 300 characters!

After the Mycenaean invasion, many Minoan Cretans took
to the mountains and high lands, and a strain of this
early race still exists in eastern Crete. Close on the Mycenaean heels came the Dorian Greeks, who founded settlements at Knossos, Gortyn and Kydonia (now Canea, or
Hania to the Greeks).

There followed centuries in which Crete was split and dis-
membered by warring factions and pirate incursions.
Around 70 B.C. Rome assumed mastery of the island,
with a capital at Gortyn (Greek: Gortis). In 826 A.D. the
Arabs invaded Crete, drove out the Romans and established
a fortress at Chandax on the north coast. This was the
forerunner of Herakleion, which up to the Middle Ages was
called Candia. A century later Byzantine forces invaded
and took over the island which, after further vicissitudes,
came into the hands of the Venetian princes. As in other
islands, the Venetians built powerful forts, and held
Crete till the mid-17th, parts of it to the early 18th
century.

The next invaders, inevitably, were the Turks. Like the
Venetians before, they were at first received as liberators,
then bloodily resented. After some violent uprisings, Crete
was given an autonomous status under Turkish rule (1898).
In 1912/1913 Crete became part of united Greece. Some
ten years later about 11,000 Turks left the island, and some
13,000 Greeks entered it from Asia Minor. This brief
period of peace was shattered by World War II, when Crete
was the scene of some of the fiercest fighting in the Mediterranean between German, and British and Greek forces.
The Germans took the island after a ten-day airborne invasion, but at such a fearful cost in casualties that Hitler
never again used this tactic in a major operation.

After the War, Crete became for a time an international
venue of scientists, archaeologists and art historians from
the U.S.A., Britain, Germany, etc. But at first it seemed
as if the mounting wave of tourism would pass it by. In
fact, right up to 1972, passengers arriving by air in

Herakleion were checked out in a series of wooden
hutments. But today, the city owns one of the most
modern airports in the Mediterranean. And where, 15
years ago you counted yourself lucky to be able to hire
a donkey as transport, today over 1,000 automobiles are
available on hire—and even one of these is hard to get! I
have the feeling that on Crete the visitor is still considered
"a guest" and has not yet deteriorated to the position of
a mere "tourist".

Staying in Crete

Earlier, there was only one starting-point for a holiday in
Crete—and that was Herakleion. Shipping agencies and
tourist offices were all crowded in the one street. Today,
there are numerous new hotels of every category. Mostly
these are in the center of the town, within bus service
of most Minoan sites. The nearest beaches are to the
east. To the west of the town are many hotels directly on
the beach.

Another modern center is Aghios Nikolaos, 44 miles east
of Herakleion. If your main interest is in bathing and
swimming facilities rather than archaeological finds, this
is the better place for you—or at one of the hotels along
Malia Bay or Mirambelou Bay, on the northern coast between Herakleion and Aghios Nikolaos. The latter is
opposite the narrowest part of the island. On the south
side of this isthmus is Ierapetra, where there are few big,
but many pleasant, smaller hotels. To the east are excellent,
secluded beaches.

The largest town in eastern Crete is Sitia, also on the north
coast, where there's plenty of accommodation, though
none so far in the luxury, A or B category. Sandy beaches
are close by.

Crete's Most Famous Beach

From Sitia, by way of the village of Palekastron, you reach
two spots of interest: to the south, the Minoan Palace of
Kato Zakros (25 miles); to the north, the celebrated beach
at Vaion (15-1/2 miles). The special thing about the latter
is the date palm wood nearby—to my knowledge unique
in Europe. According to legend, it owes its origin to a
group of Arab pirates who spat out the stones of the dates
they were eating over a large area. At any rate, it is a
delightful place to visit and the beach is equally good.

There is a great deal of camping here in summer, with young folk from throughout Europe and the U.S.A. There is a small *taverna* on the southern edge of the beach.

Centers of tourist traffic in the west of Crete are Rethimnon and Canea (Greek: Hania). Canea is the modern capital of Crete: like Herakleion, it has a daily shipping service to Piraeus: it also has an airport, with several flights daily to and from Athens. If you are traveling independently and can accept something less than first class hotel rooms, you will also find excellent accommodation in other towns, such as Hora Sfakion, Aghia Galini or Matala along the south-west coast.

'Twixt East and West: Herakleion

When, in 1912, Crete shook itself free from the Turkish yoke, many minarets were demolished as an outward sign of liberation, while old cabins and cottages grouped around Venetian forts have been swept away by new roads. But, of recent years, more care has been taken not to destroy needlessly these reminders of Crete's past.

Herakleion, former capital of Crete, under the name of Candia, was turned into one of Europe's most formidably fortified towns by Michaele Sanmichele of Verona in the 16th century. So immensely strong did he make the walls and gates that when the Turks finally attacked, it took a 22-years' siege to overcome the defenders. Candia finally capitulated in 1669, and it was not until the end of the 19th century that the Turks were finally driven out. Some of the great city gates were then taken down, but the following remain—the Porta Chania, the Porta Aghios Andrea, the Porta Kenuria, the Porta la Lazzareto.

Behind the Porta Chania is the departure point for buses for the west of the island and the Mesara Plain. On the highest of the old bastions, Martinengo, is the grave of Nikos Kazantzakis (1883-1957), poet and writer, and one of the most famous sons of Crete. His work-room is preserved in the Historical and Ethnographic Museum of Herakleion (see below). Also born in Crete were Kyriakos Theotokopoulos, better known as the painter El Greco (Spanish for "the Greek"), and Eleutherios Venizelos (1864-1936), the Cretan statesman who became Prime Minister of Greece.

For the Venetians, Candia was also an important naval port. And though the old Venetian harbor looks negligibly small beside the modern port facilities, the mighty Venetian fortress guarding the harbor shows these were not people to be trifled with.

To the west of the harbor is the popular Glass Pavilion Restaurant, and nearby the Historical and Ethnographic Museum, which is well worth a visit. In the lower rooms of the Museum are numerous pre-Christian and Byzantine statues; at ground level—frescoes and icons; on the first floor, Cretan weaving products and folk costumes, and a simulated farm kitchen of the turn of the century. Other rooms deal with more recent history.

Other spots to visit in Herakleion are:

— Morosini Fountain Square—the fountain was erected in 1628—popular cafés and guest houses are all around.

— the Metropolitan Church of Crete, dedicated to St. Titus (addressee of the unflattering remarks about Cretans in St. Paul's Epistle we have mentioned).

— Kalokerinos Street, the popular shopping street of the city.

— 1866 Street, more popularly known as the "Agora" or Market Street, a colorful precinct full of *tavernas*, where once you could eat your fill for a few pennies.

— Kornaros Square—departure point for buses to Knossos.

— King Constantine Street (Vasileos Konstantinou), contains former Turkish barracks, now municipal buildings, and some higher class shops.

— Platia Elefterias (Freedom Square)—large hotels and cafés.

— The Archaeological Museum—in its 20 rooms you can study the development of art forms from their earliest beginnings to their richest expression—a high-point are the 3,500 years-old originals of Minoan wall-paintings, mostly from the Palace of Knossos, where they have been replaced by copies.

The Palace of Knossos

A few miles south-west of Herakleion, this can be reached by buses from Kornarou Square. There are also guided

tours available, which pick up visitors from their
hotels.

The discovery and later exposure of this great palace
is owed to two great archaeologists—the German, Heinrich
Schliemann (1822-1890), and Sir Arthur Evans (see
p. 131). According to legend, Knossos had been the home
of Minos, a great and tyrannical king of Crete, who
forced the Athenians to send him yearly 7 youths and
7 maidens to be devoured by the Minotaur (half-beast,
half-man), which was kept in a labyrinth attached to his
palace. The monster was eventually overcome by Theseus
(see section on Naxos).

Schliemann had been responsible for wide discoveries
which led to the excavation of the sites of Mycenae and
Troy. He wanted to start digging at Knossos, but was
thwarted by the Turks. Evans was able to take up the
work, and over thirty years laid bare the entire foundations of the Palace. It became clear that the labyrinth
of legend was none other than the pattern of rooms in
the palace itself. Moreover, everywhere was the symbol
of the double axe, called *labrys* in Greek, so that the
palace might have been described as The House of the
Double Axe. The similarity of this word to the English
word "labyrinth" has added linguistic to historical confusion.

In an effort to show the magnificence of the original
palace, Sir Arthur Evans spent some £250,000 of his
private fortune in having it painstakingly reconstructed
in concrete (much of the Minoan original was of wood).
The reconstructed palace can be divided into three
main parts, the west wing, north entrance and the
east wing. Here are some high points of the two wings:

— West wing—magazines, small chambers containing
huge clay storage pots, the throne room;
— East wing—potters' and stone engravers' workshops,
storage rooms, royal quarters. Of great fascination to
modern visitors are the remarkably up-to-date sanitary
arrangements of 3,500 years ago.

A Trip to the Plain of Mesara

The Mesara Plain, an area south-east of Mount Idi in
central Crete, is best reached from Herakleion, either
by bus or organized tour. Many of these tours are
announced in the booklet "This Week in Crete", obtainable from Travel Offices, etc., on the island.

There are three places of interest in the area: Gortyn, site
of an early Greek settlement (on Greek maps: Gortis); the
Palace of Phaistos; ruins of the former great mansion of
Aghia Triada, where a delightful souvenir on sale is a reed-
flute made by local shepherds. Nearby are some good
bathing spots—for example, at Kokinos Pirgos, then, beyond Timbakion, at Aghia Galini. The last-named,
meaning quiet sea, has a fine, sandy beach and good facilities for accommodation: it is a half-hour's walk from
Kokinos Pirgos (stony beach).

Of interest farther south is Matala, which, some years ago,
was a haven for multi-national hippies. It has caves, steep
cliffs and a fantastic sandy beach.

From Herakleion to Canea

From Herakleion, Crete's largest city (population 60,000),
to Canea, the capital (population 40,000), is 93 odd miles.
Midway lies Rethimnon (population 17,000), Crete's third
largest city. Good bus services connect all three.

Rethimnon has a charming mixture of Venetian and Turkish
building styles. See the Venetian Loggia, now a museum,
and, above all, the great Venetian fort which towers over
the town (known locally as The Fortetza). From it, you
get a magnificent view of the White Mountains to the one
side, and the Mount Idi massif to the other.

Some 15 miles south-west of the town is the Arkadhi Monastery. In 1866, during the Wars of Liberation from Turkey,
the monastery was besieged. Sooner than surrender, the
Abbot ordered the detonation of the powder magazine,
and some 1,000 Cretans and 2,000 Turks perished. This
event is remembered throughout the island on November
8th each year. Nearby, at the village of Margarites, pottery
can be seen being made by hand.

West of Rethimnon is the long Souda Bay, now a powerful
NATO naval base. It stretches to a few miles before Canea
(on Greek maps: Hania). The old town of Canea is divided
into five areas, Chiones, Kastelli, Splanzia, Evraiki and
Topanas, each of which has an individual character. The
Archaeological Museum, containing Dorian and Minoan
relics, is in the Evraiki quarter. North-east of Canea, the
Akrotiri Peninsula offers much to see—varied countryside,
interesting caves and monasteries (especially Aghia Trias).
Some ten miles west of Canea is Maleme, with good accommodation and facilities for sub-aqua sports.

South of Canea lies the wildest, most untamed part of Crete. This is the area of the White Mountains. In the far south, between Omalos and the coast lies the Gorge of Samaria, a ravine unequalled in Europe, some 11 miles long and up to 2,000 feet deep, and varying in width between 460 feet and only 16 feet. A footpath runs all through it, but you will need strong shoes and warmer clothing than you generally wear for the beach. But for most of those who visit it, the experience is unforgettable.

Chapter Ten

THE GREEK LANGUAGE: A LITTLE HELP

Although modern Greek still has much in common with
the language spoken by Demosthenes and Pythagoras,
school classical studies won't help you much in getting
around Greece today. The fact is that Greece really has
two languages—there is *katharévussa* or High Greek and
dimotikí or Popular Greek. It's not just a question of
one being the written, the other the spoken language: the
differences go much deeper than that. *Katharévussa* is the
language of church, state and learning—of official and
juridical texts, of public notices, of the political section
of the daily newspapers. *Dimotikí* is the medium of the
everyday speech, of general news in the papers, and almost
exclusively of all branches of the arts, including film and
theater.

Generally speaking, High Greek is founded on the classical
language, while Popular Greek has assimilated many foreign
words, whether from Turkish, Latin, French or English
sources. But distinctions between the two are not always
clear-cut. Expressions given below are all from Popular
Greek.

141

The Alphabet

Always carry at least a copy of the capital letters with you,
to read notices.

How written capital	small	Name of letter	How pronounced (approximate equivalent in an English word)
A	*a*	álfa	as *a* in cart
B	β	víta	as *v* in vigor
Γ	γ	gháma	before a, o, ai, oi, it is like hard English *g* pronounced gutturally; before i, e, it is like the English *y*.
Δ	δ	<u>th</u>élta	as *th* in that
E	ε	épsilon	as *e* in ending
Z	ζ	zíta	as *z* in zipper
H	η	íta	as *ee* in street
Θ	θ	thíta	as *th* in Thursday
I	ι	ióta	as *ee* in street
K	κ	káppa	as *k* in kimono
Λ	λ	lám<u>th</u>a	as *l* in love
M	μ	mí	as *m* in mother
N	ν	ní	as *n* in never
Ξ	ξ	ksí	as *x* in fox
O	o	ómikron	as *o* in pot
Π	π	pí	as *p* in parrot
P	ρ	ró	as *r* in rotten
Σ	σ	síghma	as *s* in sight; before Greek v, m, or n, as *z* in zipper
T	τ	táf	as *t* in take
Υ	υ	ípsilon	as *ee* in street
Φ	φ	fí	as *f* in fear
X	χ	hí	before a, o, oo, like the *ch* in the Scottish "loch"; before i, e, like *h* in here, heaven
Ψ	ψ	psí	as *ps* in capsule
Ω	ω	omégha	as *o* in pot

Notes on Phonetics Used

In the following list of basic phrases, as in the alphabet
above, an attempt has been made to represent the sounds

of Greek letters by the nearest equivalent letter of the English alphabet. Where necessary to make a distinction, special measures have been taken, as follows:

Where the Greek *ghámа* is pronounced as a guttural English *g*, the phonetic printing *gh* is used; where it is pronounced like English '*y*', the character '*y*' is used. To distinguish between the hard *th* as in 'therefore' and the soft *th*, as in 'Thursday', the hard *th* is underlined, thus—<u>th</u>. Where the Greek symbol X is pronounced like the *ch* in Scottish 'loch', the English letters representing the sound are in italics, viz: ef*h*aristo (thank you); where the sound is like the English *h*, it is printed as 'h'. The small symbol ´ over a letter shows where the accent is placed: this is often very important in Greek.

Some Useful Words and Phrases

English	Approximate Greek pronunciation
how much?	póso
where?	poó
all	óli (this can have many other endings, according to the gender of the noun or nouns described)
enough	arketá
less	lighótero
many	polí, polés, polá (according to whether noun is masculine, feminine, or neuter)
more	perisótero
much, very	polí
too much	párapolí
above	epáno
below	káto
far	makryá
near	kondá
left	aristerá
right	<u>th</u>eksyá
please	parakaló
thank you	ef*h*aristó
yes	né
no	óhi

Gently, take it easy	sighá
How much does it cost?	póso káni;
I want	thélo
O.K., all right, in order	endáksi
big	meghálo
small	mikró
Good morning	kaliméra
Good evening	kalispéra
Good day or good-by	hérete
I beg your pardon (as an apology)	parndón
I don't understand you	thén sás kataláveno
Do you speak English?	ksérete anghliká;
I don't know Greek	thén kséro eliniká
Does anybody here know English?	kséri kanénas ethó anghliká;
one	énas, mia
two	thío
three	trís
four	téseris
five	pénde
six	eksi
seven	eptá
eight	októ
nine	enéa
ten	théka
eleven	éntheka
twelve	thótheka
thirteen	thekatrís
fourteen	thekatéseris
fifteen	thekapénde
sixteen	thekáksi
seventeen	thekaeftá
eighteen	thekaoktó
nineteen	thekaenéa
twenty	íkosi
twenty-one	ikosiéna

twenty-two	ikosithío
twenty-five	ikosipénde
thirty	triánda
forty	saránda
fifty	penínda
sixty	eksínda
seventy	evthomínda
eighty	oghthónda
ninety	enenínda
one hundred	ekató
two hundred	thiakósi
three hundred	trakósi
five hundred	pendakósi
one thousand	hili-i
two thousand	thío hiliáthes
one million	éna ekatomírio

There are many low-price English—Greek and Greek—English phrase books available. It will pay you to buy one from your local bookstore before setting out for Greece.

Chapter Eleven

HOW TO GET THERE

By Air

The main Greek airport is at Athens, and most of those traveling to the Greek Islands will be obliged to land there and carry on by ship or domestic flight (perhaps combined with coach or automobile), to their final destination.

There are regular flights to Athens from the following airports in the English-speaking countries listed:

United States: from Baltimore, Boston, Chicago, Cleveland, Denver, Detroit, Houston, Kansas City, Los Angeles, Miami, New York, Philadelphia, San Francisco, Washington.

Canada: from Montreal, Toronto.

Great Britain and Eire: from London, Dublin.

Australia, New Zealand, the Far East: from Brisbane, Darwin, Melbourne, Perth, Sydney, Wellington; also from Hong Kong, Singapore and numerous other centers in India and the Far East

South Africa: from Johannesburg.

147

Depending on which parts of the islands you wish to visit, other airports may be more helpful. If you wish to visit the northern Aegean Islands, for example, you will do better to fly to Thessalonica (regular flights from London, New York and numerous European cities); the island of Crete carries regular flights from London to its main city, Herakleion; the island of Corfu has regular flights from London (and Düsseldorf); the island of Rhodes (see separate book in this series), has regular flights from London.

By Sea

The main ports of entry to Greece are Piraeus (to the Greeks—Pireefs), which is the port of Athens; the town of Corfu (Kerkira), and Igoumenitsa, on the mainland nearby; Patras and Rhodes.

For visitors from North America, a number of shipping lines operate services direct from New York (Greek Line, Home Lines, American Export, etc.); alternatively, you could cross the Atlantic by regular route to a British, French, Dutch or German port, and select your onward route from there; finally, there are lines operating South Atlantic routes, which bring you to Piraeus after calling at a number of southern European ports, such as Lisbon, Gibraltar, Naples, etc.

By Rail

There are two main rail routes to Greece from London.

1. The *Direct Orient Express* leaves Victoria Station, London, each afternoon, and runs by way of Calais, Paris, Milan and the length of Yugoslavia to Thessalonica (on the third night out from London) and Athens (the following morning).

2. Each evening, a train leaves Liverpool Street Station, London, and travels by way of the Hook of Holland to connect up with the *Hellas Express* at Cologne or the *Athens Express* at Munich.

By Motor Coach

Europabus takes passengers regularly from London to Thessalonica and Athens, by way of Ostend, Brussels, Cologne, Frankfurt, Munich, Maribor and Skopje. You leave London at 21.00 hours on Friday and arrive in

Thessalonica at mid-day on Tuesday, or at Athens at 21.00 hours the same day. Service is weekly between May 31st and September 20th (1974 dates), starting each Friday. There are also other motor coach services operating from London (e.g., *European Express, Euroexpress*, etc.), on similar bases.

By Private Motor Vehicle

Europe is now criss-crossed by motorways, and there is no difficulty in reaching Greece by road. Whatever your starting point in Western Europe, your final approach is likely to be through Yugoslavia or, possibly, Albania, or by car ferry from Italy. Using the route through Yugoslavia, the distance from Calais is around 2,000 miles, and you will enter Greece either via Niki or via Evzonia. The latter entry point is the closest to Thessalonica, being some 40 miles to the north-west of the town: Niki is farther west on the Greece-Yugoslavia border. From Italy, there are car ferries to Greece from:

Venice—to the islands of Corfu or Crete, or to Piraeus;
Naples—to Piraeus;
Brindisi—to the island of Corfu, or to Igoumenitsa or Patras.

If you wish to take your own automobile to Greece, but don't want the tiring overland drive, there are *Car Sleeper Expresses* running to Milan from Paris, Ostend or Amsterdam. From Milan you can drive to Venice or Brindisi for the ferry.

If traveling by automobile, don't forget you will need the following documents: ● Vehicle Registration Book; ● International Driving Permit (not necessary for holders of a British Driving License); ● International Insurance Card (Green Card). Your motoring organization will supply details of how to obtain the latter two documents. If you wish to hire an automobile in Greece, you will need the International License.

Chapter Twelve

INFORMATION A–Z

Accommodation

All hotels in Greece are categorized—either as L (for luxury)
or A (very good), B, C, D, or E. The letter is important as
it establishes the maximum prices which may be charged—
these being fixed each year by the government. If you find
a decent-looking hotel categorized C or D, there's probably
a good reason, though it may not be obvious to you. At
the same time, you will do better to go by personal impression than by the category letter. After all, what's the use of
having the finest-looking private toilet in Europe, if it won't
flush? And, incidentally, if you find, after numerous re-
quests, that some deficiency is not corrected, you may
change your hotel and are entitled to ask for a reduction
on the bill. In this action you can ask for the help of
Greece's Tourist Police—who exercise constant vigilance
to see that every facility promised by the hotel *is* provided.

If you travel around in Greece, you will soon recognize
how great is the government's concern to increase hotel

business. In the best hotels, for example, it is generally forbidden by law to stay on any terms less than "half-pension" (i.e., bed, breakfast and a main meal). But the quality of hotel food is a different story, and I can't impress on the traveler too strongly to grasp the occasional opportunity to "eat out". Prices are very low, so even if you miss a hotel meal, you won't be much out of pocket.

If, of course, you opt for a simpler type of accommodation, problems of hotel food won't worry you (see below). But if you intend to do a good deal of traveling, especially between the islands, and prefer to stay in hotels, you will do well to get the list published annually by the Hellenic Chamber of Hotels (see ADDRESSES section). It is advisable to book well in advance, most particularly at the height of the season.

Simple and economical private accommodation is available on all the islands—in fact, on the more remote islands, it's often the only type available. As the ship docks by the quay, there are usually local people on the lookout for tourists, who will guide you to one of these guest houses. If you are traveling alone, you should note that charges are made, not so much on the basis of "one room, one charge", but according to the number of beds installed. So if you insist upon a room on your own, you may find yourself paying for two or more beds.

Aircraft Hire and Taxi Service

Under the name of *Olympic Aviation*, the Greek airline operates an air taxi service, a flight training school, and the hire of aircraft such as the Piper Cherokee-PA 28, the Piper Aztec-PA 23, etc. Hirers must, of course, possess the necessary license. For address, see ADDRESSES section.

Antiques and Antiquities

In general, antiques and works of art acquired in Greece may not be taken out of the country. Purchase of so-called "antique" icons (i.e., those over 50 years old) is only possible in certain stores licensed by the Greek Directorate of Ancient Works. The store provides a certificate which permits the purchaser to export the item.

Any attempt to take out antique works illegally is highly inadvisable: if caught, you are subject to a period of imprisonment varying from one month to five years, and to a fine of 2,000 drachmas.

In the National Archaeological Museum of Athens (approached from Patission Avenue), there is an official workshop producing copies and plaster casts of all statues on display in the museums of Greece. These may be purchased and exported without further formality.

Athens Airport

It is important to note that **Athens's Hellinikon Airport** has two widely-separated terminal buildings. On the eastern side of the airfield is a modernistic, new construction housing the foreign airline checkouts. The extensive halls on the western side are reserved for the Greek National Airline, Olympic Airways, and both domestic and international flights by "OA" are processed here. So if you are intending to land in Athens and then immediately continue by a domestic flight to one of the islands, it will certainly pay to book your flight to Greece by Olympic Airways, if this is possible. Another point: if you make a stopover in Athens and want to get back to the airport from the city, take care to tell the taxi driver which side of the airport you want, as the two parts have quite different approach roads from the city center.

Automobile Club

The Greek Automobile and Touring Club is known as ELPA, with its Head Office in Athens. It also has offices on Crete and Corfu (see ADDRESSES section).

Automobile Hire

The smaller the island, the harder you will find it to drum up a vehicle for hire. But in the main tourist centers automobile hire firms exist in droves. EOT, the Greek Tourist Organization, recommends visitors only to use the larger firms—and, of course, well-known companies like Hertz, Avis and InterRent (the Volkswagen subsidiary), are represented in Greece. Rates used to be low, but are now around the average for Central Europe. One point in passing: before accepting the vehicle, insist that the tank should be fully topped up. This will save possible friction when the bill is presented at the end.

Best Time to Visit

The islands are particularly delightful in March, April and June, when everything is green and fresh—likewise in

September and October. During July, August and September it can get very hot. One of the characteristics of the Aegean area is the *Meltemi*, a typical summer wind which repeatedly blows for several days at a time, from dawn till evening. It can cause boatmen and swimmers a lot of trouble, but at least makes the heat more bearable.

Climate

This is typically Mediterranean—long, rain-free summers and wet winters. By contrast with the mainland, extremes of temperature are less pronounced in the islands. Where the January average is 9° C. (48° F.) in Athens and 6° C. (43° F.) in Thessalonica, it is 10° C. (50°F.) for Corfu, around 12° C. (54°F.) for the Cyclades, and even slightly higher for Rhodes and Crete. Particularly in the central group of islands, strong winds are often typical: the annual average for the Cyclades lies between strengths 3 and 4 on the Beaufort scale.

It is in spring that the islands appear at their best—beginning in March and leading through May to the hot, dry summer. In July and August the heat is considerably tempered by the *Meltemi*, a very strong, north-east wind that blows at its strongest around mid-day (see **Best Time to Visit** above). Heavy showers of rain appear around the end of October: mostly they are short-lived, but can do a great deal of damage.

Here are some average air and water temperatures, for the sake of mutual comparison:

	May		June		July		August	
	C.	F.	C.	F.	C.	F.	C.	F.
Athens:	19/18	(66/64)	23/22	(73/72)	25/24	(77/75)	26/25	(79/77)
Corfu:	18/18	(64.4)	22/21	(72/70)	25/23	(77/73)	25/24	(77/75)
Crete:	20/19	(68/66)	23/23	(73.4)	24/24	(75.2)	25/25	(77.0)

Coffee

Don't be deceived by the indefinable stuff that may be served with your hotel breakfast into thinking that Greeks don't know how to make coffee. On the contrary, a decided "coffee culture" was one of the inheritances of the time of Turkish occupation, and the smallest village has its *kafenion*, its coffee shop. The brew is made from very fine powder and is served in tiny cups, accompanied by a glass of cold water. When you order, specify the degree of sweetness required, as follows (the approximate pronunciation is given, using the English alphabet):

bitter: pikró;   medium: métrio;   sweet: ghlikó.

Consulates and Embassies

See the ADDRESSES section for the addresses of main American, Australian, British, Canadian, South African and New Zealand Consulates in Greece, also the different embassies.

Customs

All used articles for personal use may be brought into Greece without payment of duty. Duty-free import also covers these goods: foodstuffs and spirits up to 10 kg. (about 22 lb.); 200 cigarettes, 50 cigars, 50 grams (about 1-3/4 ounces) of pipe tobacco, 5 boxes of matches, 2 packs of playing cards; and one each of the following: still camera, movie camera, sun spectacles, portable musical instrument, portable record player (with up to 20 discs), radio, typewriter, tape recorder, bicycle, sports equipment (skis, golf clubs, etc.). But these latter goods should be declared on entry by going through the RED lane in the Customs Office. The GREEN lane should be used if you have nothing at all to declare. Duty-free entry of these special goods is permitted, on the understanding they are for personal use and will be re-exported when the visitor leaves. Cigar smokers are particularly advised to bring the requisite stock with them, as the range on offer in Greece is somewhat limited.

New articles intended for personal use or as gifts, up to the value of 150 U.S. dollars (1974 rates), may also be imported duty-free. Goods intended for commercial trading purposes must be declared.

Documents Required

In general, no visa is required for entry into Greece. But slightly different regulations apply to the nations of the various English-speaking countries. These are as follows:

— United States, Republic of South Africa: Nationals of these countries may enter Greece for a stay of two months, without a visa, provided they have a valid passport.

— Australia, Canada, Eire, New Zealand: Nationals of
these countries may enter Greece for a stay of three months,
without a visa, provided they have a valid passport.

— Great Britain and British dependencies: British citizens
may enter Greece for a stay of three months, without a
visa, provided they have a valid British Passport or British
Visitor's Passport, issued in Great Britain (including Jersey,
Guernsey, the Isle of Man). Similar conditions apply to
nationals of the Bahamas, Bermuda, Gibraltar, etc., and
other areas under British rule.

There are, again, slightly different regulations for nationals
of the various English-speaking countries wishing to enter
Greece with their own motor vehicle, and every visitor in
this position is advised to consult his national Automobile
Association for up-to-date details. All foreign motorists
in Greece are required to have an International Driving
License, *except* holders of a British Driving License (or
Austrian, Belgian or West German license). Nationals of
other countries may obtain an International License from
ELPA (Automobile and Touring Club of Greece) on payment of 210 drachmas (1974 rates). Applicants require
their national driving license, passport, and one photograph.
Information about other documents, insurance, etc., should
be obtained from your motoring organization before leaving
for Greece. See the ADDRESSES section for the address
of the main ELPA office in Athens.

Upon entry into Greece, the vehicle owner's passport is
marked, permitting him four months' free circulation on
Greek roads. If you decide you would like to stay over
this period, you should apply to the ELPA offices in good
time for an extension.

Dress

Compared with more northerly latitudes, the Greek Islands
are, naturally, sunshine paradises. Even so, and even in the
height of summer, cooler periods do occur, and there can
be noticeable cooling-off in the evenings. So on no account
go without a supply of knitted garments.

Also, you will need more than just a pair of sunglasses to
cope with the strong sunshine. Arm yourself with the
widest-brimmed hat you can find, preferably a straw one.
If you cannot get one before you leave, you will find them
on sale throughout Greece, at reasonable prices.

A certain formality attaches to hotel mealtimes: the Greek
attaches considerable importance to a good appearance,

and this should be borne in mind when you do your packing. Finally, when visiting a church or a religious building, women should always be wearing a frock, and preferably have their heads covered (also a necessary protection against the sun). In similar circumstances, men should not be wearing shorts, or even short-sleeved attire. These are points in which it is most important to respect local custom.

Duty-free Shop

There is a duty-free shop in each of the Athens Airport terminals, where international brands of spirits, perfumes, tobacco goods, etc., may be purchased free of customs duty. Greek specialities are also on sale, though at less favorable prices.

Electric Current

In general, 220 volts AC current is in use throughout Greece. In one or two places, and especially on the older ships, you will still find 110 volts being used.

Feasts and Festivals

These play an important part in Greek life. Most have a religious basis. As soon as you arrive in a locality it is worth your while to enquire if there will be any festivals in the area during the period of your stay: most are worth a considerable journey to see. The following list gives a small selection of major feast days and festivals throughout Greece.

January 1: New Year's Day, the feast of St. Basil (St. Vassillios to the Greek);

January 6: feast of the Epiphany (Theophania);

February–March: carnival time throughout the country, but especially in the *Plaka* quarter of Athens, in Patras and on Cephallonia;

March 25: Feast of the Annunciation and National Day, with military parades. On Tinos Island, a pilgrimage to Mary's icon; on Kasos, drama performances in the villages;

Easter: the high point of the Orthodox Church's liturgical calendar. It should be noted that the Eastern Orthodox Church's calculation of the date of Easter generally falls a little before that of the western churches. On the Orthodox Good Friday there are processions from every church, preceded by the *epitaphios* or pall: on Easter Saturday there is the service of Christ's Resurrection at night, followed by a traditional meal including *magiritsa* (a tripe soup) and tinted eggs: Easter Sunday is the crown of the feast, with outdoor celebrations, folk-dancing, lambs roasted on spits, etc.

April 30: the feast of Saint George.

May 1: especially celebrated in and around the larger cities;

May 21: feast of St. Constantine and St. Helen;

May 29: at Canea (Chania) on Crete, a celebration of the anniversary of the Battle for Crete in 1941; sports events, exhibitions, etc., called *Venizeleia*: Feast of the Ascension of Christ; celebrations throughout Greece, the date being dependent on the date fixed for Easter that year.

July—August: the Athens Festival of Music and Drama, with presentations of ancient drama in the Herod Atticus Theater, at the foot of the Acropolis;

Throughout August: an ancient Cretan marine festival takes place at Canea on Crete.

August 11: Procession of St. Spiridon on Corfu;

August 15: the feast of the Assumption of the Virgin, a popular religious festival: on Tinos, a popular pilgrimage to a miraculous icon of Mary; at Malia, on Crete, a water-melon feast; at Pythagorian on Samos, a great wine festival;

September 8: on Spetsaï Island, a festival in memory of the defeat of the Turkish fleet;

Mid-September: Feast of the Grape at Herakleion in Crete.

October 28: National Day to commemorate Greece's historical "No" (*ochi*) to the Axis Powers in 1940.

November 11: on Chios there is a celebration to mark the anniversary of liberation from Turkish rule.

December 24-25: Christmas celebrations;

December 31: New Year's Eve, with all-night merry-making, mostly with a family background.

Food and Drink

Whereas the hotels seem to vie in producing a uniform kind of so-called "international cuisine", you can eat very well in the popular taverns or better restaurants. Greek cooking is a somewhat coarser descendant of the finer Turkish

cuisine—which, it its turn, derives from Byzantine Greek. The Greek cook's addiction to olive oil has given his dishes an undeservedly bad reputation. If you are one of those who finds this ingredient offensive to the stomach, arm yourself with some charcoal tablets or ask your pharmacist for a suitable preparation.

On the islands, fish and sea-food dishes generally are of superb quality—especially various types of lobster, known as *astakós* or *karavides*, and cuttle-fish (*kalamarákia*). In summer, the main dish is mutton or lamb, and anyone who is prejudiced against this particular meat should abandon his distaste. Pork, too, can be delightfully prepared, also beef in various casserole forms, such as *kokkinistó*. *Soovláki* is the name for small cubes of meat grilled on a skewer. A universal dish is spaghetti, generally prepared *à la Bolognèse*.

Most menus will be prepared with an English translation. If in difficulties, go directly to the serving table or to the kitchen itself, to see what is being prepared.

Whatever happens, don't neglect to have a dessert. This will generally consist either of delicious, fresh island fruits or of very sweet delicacies. And when it's time to pay, you will get another pleasant surprise. Even after a real gourmet feast, the charge will not be excessive.

To start with the wines, there are two main varieties to choose from—resinated (*retsína*) and unresinated (*aretsínoto*). This distinction dates right back to ancient times, when some means had to be found of conserving wine for long periods. The solution was to smear the containers with resin from the Aleppo pine. This was found to give the wine a distinctive flavor and (allegedly) greater wholesomeness. So, to this day, popular table wines in Greece remain resinated. Here, again, there is a choice between a bottled, commercial product and the local island wine, which comes straight from the cask to the table. The latter kind is better, but tends to be uneven in strength and is gradually taking second place. The bottled *retsína*, however, is also good, and sound value for money.

But this is by no means to denigrate the unresinated Greek wines. On the contrary, even simple table wines taste splendid. In gourmet establishments you can get top brands, but still at relatively low prices.

Among spirituous drinks, the following are the most common: good Greek brandy (*konyák*), the two spirits known as *raki* and *tsipuro*, but most of all, *ouzo*, the ubiquitous aperitif with its aniseed flavor. *Ouzo* is served mixed with water, which then turns milky, and very often with a salad side-plate of olives and/or tomatoes, small snails and morsels of cuttle-fish and cheese. This side plate is known as a *mesé*, but the practice of serving it with drinks is, unfortunately, steadily becoming rarer, at least in the areas most frequented by tourists: you may have to hunt around to find the place serving the best *mesé*.

Beer is also important to Greeks. In the days of the first King Otto, a German brewer named Fuchs made his way from Munich to Athens, and started selling his product as "Fix"—which is a lot easier for a Greek to pronounce. But there are numerous other brewing companies: Henniger, for instance, has a large subsidiary at Herakleion in Crete. Generally speaking, you will find only bottled beer, the favorite size being the half litre (about 9/10 of a pint). One advantage of beer is that it makes the drinker less tired than wine, and can sometimes be drunk throughout the day. Its disadvantage is that it goes less well than wine (and especially *retsína*) with the predominantly oily Greek food.

Gaming

There are two casinos on the islands—one in the Achilleion (former Imperial) Palace on Corfu, one in the Grand Hotel of Rhodes city. Roulette and Chemin-de-fer are played in both. The latter is a game for more advanced players, but roulette is simpler, and in the gaming rooms you will be given a leaflet explaining the more important rules.

Golf

There is an 18-hole course at Livadi tou Ropa, about 7-8 miles outside Corfu town. There is also an 18-hole course on Rhodes, opened in 1973.

Greek Art History

There are four main periods of ancient Greek art and architecture, named as follows:

The Geometric Period — from about 1100 B.C. to 700 B.C.

The Archaic Period — from about 700 to 475 B.C.; this covers three periods: the Oriental — to about 550 B.C.; the Middle Archaic — from 550 to 515 B.C.; the Late Archaic — from 515 to 475 B.C.

The Classical Period — from about 475 B.C. to 323 B.C.; this also covers three periods: Early Classical — 475-448 B.C.; Middle Classical — 448-400 B.C.; Late Classical — 400-323 B.C.

The Hellenistic Period — from about 323 to 31 B.C.

Varied architectural forms characterize each period.

From about 625 B.C., we find *Doric* columns in use. These have no base, a slightly tapering shaft and 16—20 vertical channelings; their main point of origin is the Greek mainland, especially the Peloponnese.

From about 570 B.C., *Ionic* columns appear; these have richly molded circular bases and a slenderer column rising to a voluted capital; main point of origin is Asia Minor and its off-shore islands.

From the 4th century B.C., the *Corinthian* column appears: this has a slender shaft and an ornately-designed capital, with leaves and volutes.

Some high points in Greek art development are:

Archaic Period: the great Greek sculptures begin to appear from the second half of the 7th century B.C. on: around 600 B.C. there is a preference for over-life-size figures, as at Naxos and Delos.

Early Classical Period: the high point in representational sculpture of the human figure (temple of Aphaia on Aegina).

Middle Classical Period: Athens is the artistic center for this period.

Late Classical Period: the first portrait statues.

The Hellenistic Period: detailed sculptural studies of highly individualized persons: Rhodes develops as a center of the arts.

Roman Period: 146 B.C. to 395 A.D.: emergence of the Rhodes school of sculpture.

Byzantine Period: A.D. 395 to 1494: erection of numerous churches and religious buildings, often with significant frescoes and mosaics (Néa Móni on Chios, Hekaton Piliani on Paros, the catacombs of Melos). The Byzantine Orthodox churches are mostly churches with cruciform domes: the base is in the form of a Greek cross, with the cupola erected over the intersection of the four equal-length arms.

Insects

As in most south European areas, gnats and midges present a problem—especially in the more remote islands, where measures to combat these pests are not so extensive as elsewhere. On the beach, one of the best ways of keeping them at bay is by smoking a cigarette. But you should arm yourself in advance with some remedy for possible stings or bites, obtained from your local pharmacist.

Much less pleasant are insects in the bedroom—though it must be said that in the tourist centers this is largely a thing of the past. But if you should face this problem, ask the porter or proprietor for some "Moon Tiger". This is a Japanese product, a type of spiral which smoulders for several hours, and keeps the intruders at bay. The following morning you will be able to buy a whole packet of them at the nearest store for a few drachmas.

Kiosk Stores

At almost every corner, and along the pavements in Greece you will find a *peripteron*, or kiosk. These are superstores in miniature, selling a huge range of small goods, from cigarettes, chocolates and candies to newspapers and magazines (in larger centers, in many languages), maps and guide books, stamps and writing materials, photographic requisites, sewing and mending materials, aspirins, sun cream, and so on and so on.

One advantage of these little stores is that they are not bound by normal opening hours, and are generally open from early morning to late at night, including Sundays and holidays. Most kiosks also have a telephone, from which you may make a local call for 2 drachmas.

Local Time

Clocks in Greece go by Eastern European time—which is two hours ahead of Greenwich Mean Time. This means that when it is 12 noon in Greece, it will be 10 a.m. GMT, and 11 a.m. in Central Europe, and you will need to adjust your watch accordingly when entering and leaving the country.

Mail

Stamps are sold in post offices, hotels and kiosks. The postal service abroad is quite fast: current rates (1974) are similar to those in most western countries. "Poste Restante" facilities are generally available, if you wish them.

Money

The unit of currency in Greece is the *drachma*, which is further divided into 100 *lepta*. Although the lepta has ceased to have much significance, there are 5, 10, 20 and 50 lepta coins still in circulation. Mainly in use are coins of 1, 2, 5 and 10 drachmas and notes for 50, 100, 500 and 1,000 drachmas. The former silver 20 drachma coin has now been withdrawn. Bank note colors are as follows: 50—blue, 100—red, 500—green, 1,000—rust color. In English, drachma is sometimes written *dr.* and sometimes *dma.*; in the plural it is often written *drx.*

Exchange-wise, you will do best to buy your drachmas on arrival in Greece—against banknotes or travelers' checks. No limit is imposed by Greece on the amount of your own currency you import—though, of course, this may be restricted by your country of origin. Exchange facilities exist everywhere—at border posts, at the airport, and, of course, in the banks. It is advisable to bring a small sum in drachmas with you, for tips, taxi fares, etc.

News in English

The Greek National Broadcasting and Television Institution (EIRT) broadcasts a news bulletin in English at 8.10 a.m. and 21.45 h. over the radio, and at 21.55 h. on television.

Nude Bathing

Naturists should be warned that bathing in the nude is not regarded with *official* favor anywhere in Greece—though the celebrated beaches of Mykonos are an exception, where the practice is silently tolerated. Anywhere else, and police intervention is likely! But anyone who looks at the enormous extent of Greek beaches must realize there are plenty of places where nobody is likely to object to your bathing in the nude—for the simple reason there *is* nobody for miles around.

Orthodox Church

In the year 1054, Pope Leo IX's advisor, Cardinal Humbert, excommunicated the then Patriarch of Constantinople. This led to the so-called Great Schism, the final separation of Christendom into the Roman and Eastern Orthodox persuasions. The respective areas of influence of the two branches of the Christian Church of those days were further determined by the division of the Holy Roman Empire into Eastern and Western sections. In this connection, let us remember the historic embrace of the Pope of Rome and the Greek Orthodox Patriarch in 1967.

Shoe-Shine Boys

As in southern countries generally, Greece is the home of countless shoe-shine boys—so many, in fact, you wonder how they all make a living. But great emphasis is placed upon having shiny, bright shoes. Moreover, you will not find shoes are anywhere cleaned in the hotels, so it's pointless to leave them outside your door at night. Going price (1974) for a street shine: 5 drachmas a pair.

Sub-Aqua Sports

Although the clarity of the sea facilitates any underwater sport, under-sea fishing with compressed air equipment is only permitted in certain areas. Likewise, it is forbidden to harpoon any creature below 150 grams (about 5-1/4 ounces) in weight. Any underwater fishing must be carried out at least 100 meters (about 100 yards) distant from fishermen's nets or the nearest shore.

There are diving schools in many of the major tourist centers. In the Rhodes area, such a school is conducted on a ship which anchors each evening in Mandraki Harbor (about 50 miles north of Rhodes), and you can make enquiries and/or register as a pupil there.

Telephone

Telephone services in Greece are in the hands of the O.T.E., the Greek Telecommunications Organization. With its aid, you can telephone automatically to almost any part of the country and also to a number of foreign countries. English-speaking countries which can be reached from Greece by automatic dialing, with their appropriate prefix code, are as follows: United States — 001; Canada — 001; Great Britain or Eire — 0044.

You may call a country not on the automatic dialing network through the International Exchange operator, whose number is 160 or 161. Compared with the tariffs of other European countries, Greek telephone services are cheap. The Head Office of the O.T.E. is in Athens, but there are sub-offices in towns and even the larger villages. In main tourist centers there is generally a switchboard manned throughout the 24 hours. If you are calling internationally, be prepared for a wait: central European lines tend to become overloaded.

Calling a number within the Greek domestic network is simple. Here is a selection of code prefixes which may be useful:

Aegina	— 0297	Moudros	
Andros	— 0282	(Limnos)	— 0276
Argostoli	— 0871	Mykonos	— 0235
Athens	— 021	Myrina	
Canea (Crete)	— 0821	(Limnos)	— 0276
Chalkis (Euboea)	— 0221	Mytilene	
Chios	— 0271	(Lesbos)	— 0276
Corfu	— 0661	Naxos	— 0285
Herakleion		Rhodes	— 0241
(Crete)	— 081	Salamis	— 021
Hydra (see Ydra)		Samos	— 0273
Ierapetra (Crete)	— 0842	Skiathos	— 0424
Kimi (Euboea)	— 0222	Spetsai	— 0298
Kos	— 0242	Syra	— 0281
Mallia (Crete)	— 0897	Thasos	— 0593
Melos	— 0287	Tinos	— 0282
		Ydra (or Hydra)	— 0248

Tipping

In almost all hotels and restaurants you will now find your bill is presented with a 15 per cent service charge already included. But you may like to give a small extra consideration to one or more of these: the baggage porter (assuming one is available, and you've used his services), when you arrive and when you leave; the room maid, generally a charming person, when you leave—or, if you're staying for a longer period, from time to time; finally, according to his friendliness and helpfulness, the door porter, in establishments where the proprietor himself doesn't control the keys. In restaurants, a head waiter who has served or advised you well will be grateful for a small remuneration (about 5 per cent of the totals). But, under no circumstances,

forget to reward the *mikros*, the little lad who brings you
bread and drinks. He will receive no regular wage, but is
entirely dependent on your tip: you should give him from
5 to 10 drachmas, according to the size of your meal. If
you wish to summon him, call "mikré". Leave his tip on
the table, not on the plate on which the bill is presented, or
the head waiter will take it.

Toilets

In most parts of Greece, public toilets are marked either
with customary picture symbols, or with English names.
Where this is not the case, try to remember the following
Greek symbols:

LADIES   = ΓΥΝΑΙΚΩΝ   (pronounced *yinekón*)

GENTLEMEN = ΑΝΔΡΩΝ   (pronounced *anthron*,
                                            with hard "*th*")

There are various expressions, if you wish to find the
nearest toilet, as follows:

Where is the toilet?   *poo ine í tooaléta;*

Where is the lavatory?   *poo ine tó apohoritírio;*

A simpler expression, especially in country districts is:
poo ine tó meros; Meros simply means "the place". The
semi-colon (;), is the symbol used by Greeks as a question
mark—i.e. it is the equivalent of (?).

Tourist Information Offices

The National Tourist Organization of Greece is the
Ellinikós Organismós Turismu, abbreviated to E.O.T.
This is the official agency responsible for all tourist ques-
tions. Its main office is in Athens, but there is a branch in
all the larger towns of the country, as well as in principal
cities of foreign countries. See the ADDRESSES section.
Staff in all offices will be able to speak English and some
other foreign languages. E.O.T. is approximately pronounced "ay-ot" (with "ay" as in "day").

Tourist Police

A wise institution in Greece, the job of the Tourist Police
is to ensure that any regulations affecting tourists are ob-
served. In addition, they find accommodation, advise in

any travel question, listen to complaints. Although invariably friendly types, few of them speak any foreign language. But, in Greece, communication always seems somehow possible, despite the language barrier.

Traffic Regulations

Common international traffic regulations are in force in Greece. When entering a European-style traffic roundabout, it's important to note that traffic approaching from the right, that is, vehicles *entering* the roundabout have the right of way. Maximum speed on highways and national routes is 110 km/hr. (68 m.p.h.). Sounding the horn is generally forbidden in built-up areas. Any indulgence in alcohol is strictly forbidden to drivers.

Travel Between the Islands

Basically, there are two main ways of traveling between the islands—fast ways and not-so-fast ways. The fast way, of course, is by aircraft. There are flights to and from the following island destinations:

Corfu, Levkas (landing at Aktion, close by on the mainland), Cephallonia, Zakynthos, Cythera, Crete (Herakleion and Canea—sometimes spelt as Chania or Hania), Karpathos, Rhodes, Kos, Melos, Mykonos, Samos, Chios, Lesbos, Limnos, Skiathos, Thasos (via mainland Kavala), Samothrace (via mainland Alexandroupolis), and Spetsaï (via mainland Porto Cheli).

Flight schedules to the major islands are quite heavy—but owing to the cheapness of the fares, passenger loading is equally heavy, and it is essential to book your place in advance. The low cost of Greek domestic flights comes as a pleasant surprise.

The not-so-fast means of travel is by ship or boat. In this connection, Piraeus is pre-eminently the central port for Greek commercial and tourist sea traffic. There is, literally, no island which cannot be reached from this center. At the same time, it's not always a rapid procedure. First, you must find a ship going where you want to go, then you must wait for it to sail.

The Greek Tourist Organization, E.O.T., regularly publishes fresh timetables, but the unavoidable delays which occur soon make these out of date. If you wish to use this means of travel, arm yourself in advance with a "Key Travel Guide for Greece and the Middle East", obtainable at any kiosk in Greece, or from the address given in the ADDRESSES section of this book. You will be able to consult a copy at the Greek National Tourist Organization of your country of origin.

This "Key Guide" lists the main shipping routes between the mainland and the islands. The Ionian Islands (especially Corfu), Igoumenitsa, Patras and (via the Corinth Canal) Piraeus, can be conveniently reached from Brindisi in Italy. For Andros and the other northern Cyclades, the best connections are from the small harbors in the south-east of Attica (e.g. Rafina) and in the south-east of Euboea (Karistos).

Kimi, at a mid-point on the east coast of Euboea, is the center for a shipping line connecting the northern Sporades (Skiros, Skiathos, etc.) with the mainland center of Volos.

Twice a week a ship leaves Thessalonica for Herakleion in Crete, stopping at various islands of the northern Cyclades group (i.e. Tinos, Mykonos, Santorini, etc.).

The northern Aegean islands of Samothrace and Thasos can best be reached by ship from Kavala or Alexandrou-polis on the Greek mainland.

In general, travel by ship offers good value for money—though it is unwise to expect all the comforts of a luxury liner.

Much local traffic between islands is carried out by the ubiquitous *caïques*. One of these will certainly take you to your destination at low cost. But you should remember they are fairly lightly built and not the best form of transport when seas are running high. But, on the other hand, sea-sickness is equally common on a large liner, amongst those who are prone to it. If you know yourself to be a poor sailor, take care to arm yourself in advance with suitable tablets from your local drugstore.

Water

On the islands, drinking water is practically sacred, due to its relative scarcity. When a glass of water is served with your meal or coffee, drink it with some reverence—realizing its value as a commodity! Added to which, you will generally find it of superlative taste.

Chapter Thirteen

ADDRESSES

Foreign Consulates

The consulates and/or embassies of the main English-speaking countries in Greece are as follows (given in alphabetical order):

E— *Embassy;* C—*Consulate*

Australia (E/C)
    8 Makedonon St., Athens; tel: 6425310 and 6425316

Canada (E/C)
    4 Ioannou Genadiou St., Athens; tel: 739511

Great Britain (E)
    1 Ploutarchou-Ypsilantou St., Athens; tel: 736211

Great Britain (C)
    24 Akti Possidonos, Piraeus; tel: 4178345

New Zealand (C)
    29 Leoforos Vasilissis Sofias Ave., Athens; tel: 727515

Republic of South Africa
69 Leoforos Vasilissis Sofias Ave., Athens; tel: 729050

United States of America (E/C)
91 Leoforos Vasilissis Sofias Ave., Athens; tel: 712951

Tourist Offices

The Head Office of E.O.T., the National Tourist Organiza-
tion of Greece, is at: 2 Amerikis St., Athens; tel: 3223111.
E.O.T. has main subsidiary offices in: Canea (Crete);
Yannina; Herakleion (Crete); Kavala; Corfu; Larissa; Patras;
Thessalonica; Volos; Rhodes; Kos; Igoumenitsa.

The main offices in English-speaking countries are: Great
Britain: 195/197 Regent St., London W.1; United States:
601 Fifth Ave., New York 1007; 627 West Sixth St., Los
Angeles, Calif.

Hellenic Chamber of Hotels

Located at: 20 Amerikis St., Athens; tel: (21) 634 728,
this organization publishes an annual list of hotel accommodation, under the title "Guide to Greek Hotels".

"Key Travel Guide" Boat Timetables

The "Key Travel Guide for Greece and the Middle East",
published from 6 Kriezotou St., Athens, lists all major
sailings between the Greek mainland and Greek islands.

Automobile Club of Greece

The Greek Automobile & Touring Club is known as ELPA.
Head office is at 2-4 Messogion St., Tower of Athens; tel:
7791615; telex: 215-763. There is a branch office at Canea
on Crete: 6 Verovitz Pasha; at Herakleion on Crete: Platia
Eleftheriou Venizelou; in Rhodes town; and in Kerkira
town on Corfu; as well as in the mainland towns of Thessalonica, Volos, Patras, Larissa and Kavala.

Aircraft Hire and Taxi Services

The address of Olympic Aviation, whose services are described under the title above, in the INFORMATION A—Z
section, is: Hellenikon Airport, Athens; tel: (21) 9813 565.

Chapter Fourteen

SOME FURTHER READING
AND A LAST WORD

For those who would like to do some further reading before going on holiday, the following is a list of books bearing on travel in the Greek Islands. This list makes no claims to being comprehensive, nor does inclusion or exclusion of any book imply either recommendation or its opposite. All the books listed are personal accounts by the authors concerned, but very few cover the whole of the Greek Islands as comprehensively as the pages you have just read.

Recommended and quoted by the author is Ernle Bradford's "The Greek Islands", published by Collins, London, in their "Companion Guide" series (1964).

"The Aegean—A Sea-Guide to Its Coasts and Islands" by H.M. Denham, published by John Murray, London (1970). This book is specifically aimed to help those who intend to tour the Aegean Islands under sail, and is based on personal experience.

"Aegean Quest—A Search for Venetian Greece" by Eric Forbes-Boyd, published by Dent, London (1970).

"The Ionian Islands—Zakynthos to Corfu" by Arthur Foss, published by Faber and Faber, London (1969).

"Gates of the Wind" by Michael Carroll, published by John Murray, London (1965). Concerns the Northern Sporades.

"Some Greek Islands" by Joseph Braddock, published by Robert Hale, London (1967). Concerns Lesbos, some of the Cyclades, Paros, Naxos, Ios, Santorin, Mykonos, Delos, Rhodes, Aegina, Salamis, Athens and Corfu.

"The Isles of Greece" by Robert Payne, published by Hamish Hamilton, London (1965).

"Rhodes—Get to know it—Get to like it" by Frank Weimert, is no. 11 in this series by Interauto Book Co. Ltd., London, and Drake Publishers Inc., New York.

Two books on Crete, recommended by the author, have been written by John Bowman and Robin Bryans respectively.

Most of the above books are British publications, but many of them will be equally obtainable outside the British Isles. If in doubt, ask your local bookshop or lending library. Generally speaking, they are intended for reading before you go on holiday, rather than to take with you. The author's advice is: travel light; don't try to do all the islands in a single summer! Happy Islanding!

INDEX

Bold type indicates the name of an island which has a section in this book; alternative names are in brackets.